Factoring

Melvyn Westlake

Pitman Publishing

First published 1975

PITMAN PUBLISHING LTD
Pitman House, 39 Parker Street, London WC2B 5PB, UK

PITMAN MEDICAL PUBLISHING CO LTD
42 Camden Road, Tunbridge Wells, Kent TN1 2QD, UK

FOCAL PRESS LTD
31 Fitzroy Square, London W1P 6BH, UK

PITMAN PUBLISHING CORPORATION
6 East 43 Street, New York, NY 10017, USA

FEARON PUBLISHERS INC
6 Davis Drive, Belmont, California 94002, USA

PITMAN PUBLISHING PTY LTD
Pitman House, 158 Bouverie Street, Carlton, Victoria 3053, Australia

PITMAN PUBLISHING
COPP CLARK PUBLISHING
517 Wellington Street West, Toronto M5V 1G1, Canada

SIR ISAAC PITMAN AND SONS LTD
Banda Street, PO Box 46038, Nairobi, Kenya

PITMAN PUBLISHING CO SA (PTY) LTD
Craighall Mews, Jan Smuts Avenue, Craighall Park,
Johannesburg 2001, South Africa

ISBN 0 273 00070 5

Text set in 10/11 pt. Monotype Times New Roman, printed by letterpress, and bound in Great Britain at The Pitman Press, Bath

B.904:43

Preface

It is quite usual in books of this type for the author to express his appreciation for the assistance he has received in its preparation. Without the forbearance, helpfulness and, frequently, the active support, of many people within the factoring industry, this book could certainly not have been written. Because factoring has only comparatively recently emerged as a financial service in Europe, there were—at least when I began writing on the subject—no previous texts in Britain to draw upon. Much of the material herein was gleaned from interviews with the senior management of factoring companies and first-hand observation of their operations. A factor writing about his own industry could doubtless have brought greater authority to the topic. I hope that my contribution may, coming from a neutral observer, bring the greater objectivity that comes with being uninvolved.

For the legal and historical background I have drawn, in part, upon published American material, and would like to make acknowledgements to Roy A. Foulke, author of an expanded essay called *The Story of the Factor;* and Roscoe T. Steffen and Frederick S. Danziger who wrote *The Rebirth of the Commercial Factor*, a 'special bulletin' published by the Division of Research & Publications, at the National Conference of Commercial Receivable Companies, Inc.

I have chosen to use the word 'financer' when a general term was required to embrace a variety of lending institutions (factor/company lending on security/invoice discounting company/bank). It is a word widely used in the U.S. but found in few British dictionaries. However, it is preferable to the word 'financier' which has acquired connotations that do not accurately convey the meaning I seek to express.

To allow for easy comparison I have tended to quote many figures in dollars, except when discussing the domestic British situation. Currency conversions have been made at the parities agreed at the Smithsonian Institute in December 1971.

M.W.

Contents

1 *The Function of the Factor*

Factoring is both a financial technique and a management service. It is a method of converting a passive asset into an active agent of commercial growth. In part, it is an answer to the increasing complexity and specialization of modern business. Developing as a response to such influences, factoring, together with other new financial techniques such as leasing, has established itself as an important tool for the husbanding of scarce resources.

For many companies, cash is a scarcer resource than it need be because they have to wait too long to receive payment for goods and services they have provided. It is little consolation for a company to be able to include amounts due from debtors as a large current asset in its balance sheet; much better to sell that asset for cash which can immediately be put to productive use. A factor makes that transaction possible.

In essence, a factor buys book-debts arising from the normal conduct of trade, in the same way that other companies might purchase pig-iron, cotton cloth or molasses. This purchase of debts is central to the function of factoring, permitting the factor to provide three basic services: the immediate advance of funds against the debts he agrees to buy; the underwriting of the credit risk involved in such unpaid debts; and the administration of the vendor's sales ledger. The company selling the debts is known as the factor's 'client'.

A factor may provide all three services or various combinations of them. Precisely which arrangement a factor's client chooses, is largely dependent on his requirements. Frequently, but by no means exclusively, his principal need is simply money. Most often, the provision of finance will entail the factor also administering the sales ledger as this ensures greater control over the quality and recoverability of the underlying debts, upon which the finance is extended.

All of the services rendered by a factor can be obtained from other sources. Computer bureaux provide sales ledger accounting facilities; specialist credit insurance companies exist to underwrite trade credit risks. The debt collection function, which the factor also naturally assumes, is often executed by collection agencies. Trade debts, too, can be used as collateral to raise funds from some financial institutions. Banks have long been engaged in this form of lending. But the factor uniquely brings all those services together in one package. The actual

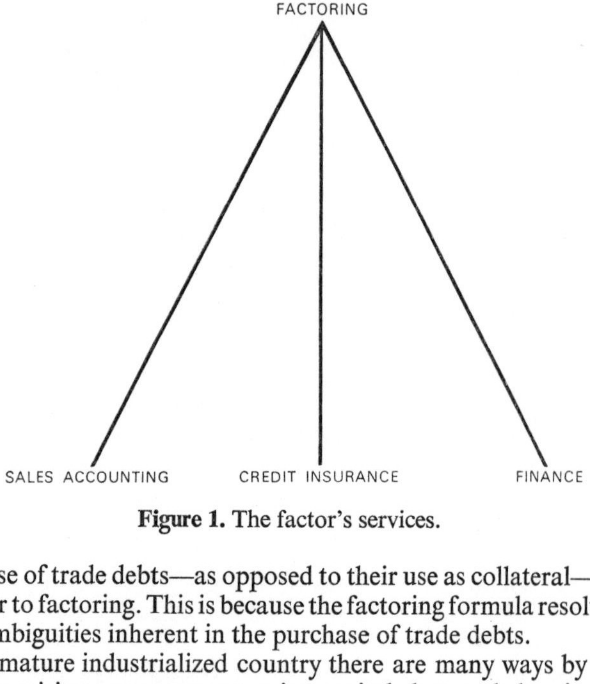

Figure 1. The factor's services.

purchase of trade debts—as opposed to their use as collateral—is also singular to factoring. This is because the factoring formula resolves the legal ambiguities inherent in the purchase of trade debts.

In a mature industrialized country there are many ways by which an enterprising company can raise capital, but each has its price, which may, in some cases, be geared to the ultimate use of the funds. For its part, factoring offers a distinct solution to the problems posed by capital tied up in trade debts. When money is outstanding for 60 or 90 days this means either that more capital is deployed in the business than would be dictated simply by the production cycle, or that expansion is being retarded because insufficient funds are left for production.

Commonly one-fifth of a company's annual turnover is outstanding in the form of trade debts. This clearly signifies a wasting asset. The cashflow is slowed down, creating illiquidity problems which can endanger the solvency of a company and cause considerable concern to management. Even in its less harmful form it is an expensive use—or misuse—of funds, frequently contributing to the growth of the customer rather than the supplier. At worst, it can lead to a cash crisis that might prove terminal. Commercial history is strewn with spectacular company failures, at least partially due to this kind of financial thrombosis.

Additionally, considerable credit risks are run by a company with a large portfolio of debts. It is estimated that when Rolls Royce, Upper Clyde Shipbuilders and Lines Bros (the Meccano toy and baby carriage manufacturers) collapsed in 1971, they owed a total of some £250 million in trade debts to suppliers. The effect of this on a number of suppliers was traumatic, with many of them incurring large losses from the wholesale writing-off of these debts. This demonstrates the inter-locking nature of the factor's second service—credit insurance—with the provision of funds.

If a company is to avoid the financially suspect customer, it requires first-class information about other companies within its industry. It also needs trained full-time credit controllers. Many companies cannot afford credit managers, and so this function is the part-time responsibility of the sales executive. Often, there is an inherent conflict between the sales and credit departments over the volume of credit that might be permitted to a valued customer. The credit intelligence at the factor's disposal endows him with an almost unequalled capacity to assess, advise and, usually, accept, the credit risks involved.

It follows that if the factor advances funds and takes the credit risk, control of the sales ledger is a natural third leg of the trifurcate factoring function. Accounting records must be accurate up to date, and maintained in such a manner that information is readily accessible and identifiable at any moment in time. Statements must be prepared and distributed regularly each month. Returns must be dealt with promptly to ensure that credit notes are issued speedily and disputes settled. Overdue accounts must be identified and collections made discreetly, with the minimum of acrimony. The factor's administration of the sales ledger should normally result in a considerable improvement in the standard and efficiency of this operation, together with a faster cashflow. Typically, the cashflow might improve by 15 per cent.

However, in no sense does this adoption of the sales ledger by the factor mean that the management of the client relinquishes ultimate control. It remains master of the business. Rather, it is being relieved of a management chore. Clearly, no financial institution will invest money without some safeguard, but where a good client-factor relationship is established, the usual protective checks are unlikely to prove onerous. Where the client is a manufacturer, for example, the

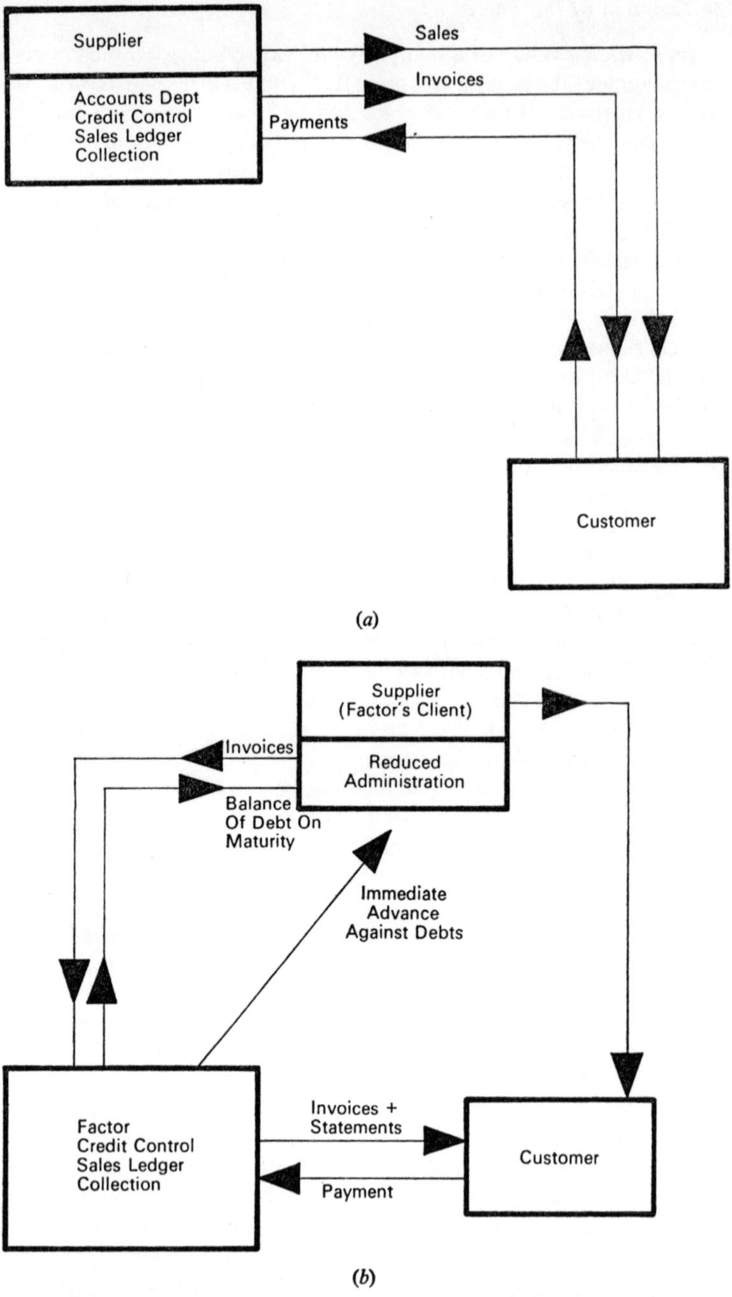

Figure 2. (*a*) Normal trade sequence (*b*) Factoring procedure.

business of winning orders and producing goods remains firmly the responsibility of the management.

Neither does the factor advance 'last resort' funds to financially unhealthy companies unable to obtain regular lines of finance from banks and other sources. This was the case in the early, formative years of factoring in Britain. In an endeavour to win recognition for their services, factors have been guilty of accepting doubtful and unsound clients, to the detriment of the factoring industry as a whole. This badly tarnished its reputation, and it has taken a considerable time to recover from this loss of respectability.

Today, in theory, the factor is interested only in companies with good growth potential and competent management, which can benefit from its services. Then, the client and factor both prosper from such a relationship. Conversely, a shrinking client will inevitably find the costs involved progressively more burdensome, while the factor will probably find the operation progressively less remunerative. Factoring like other financial techniques, is not suitable for universal application. It is appropriate in certain situations and at a particular phase of a company's development. The benefits must be set against the relatively high cost, and the advantages weighed carefully.

It is the small and medium-sized companies that benefit most from factoring. Some large public enterprises also factor their debts, but frequently this is in the realm of international trade, where credit evaluation and debt collection present very distinct problems. Companies with less than 100 employees still account for over 40 per cent of the working population in Britain. For them, internal funds—those derived mainly from retentions of past profits—are the most important source of finance. Private companies tend to retain a greater percentage of their profits than public companies.

Similarly, trade credit is a proportionately larger item in the accounts of small firms. Many rely on trade credit, which can often be a convenient form of finance. But excessive use involves overtrading (expansion without adequate liquid assets). Often these companies are in turn extending considerable credit to their own suppliers.

There are, of course, a number of ways in which the funds employed in a business can be increased. A company may make a public issue of shares, but this can be expensive if a relatively small sum is required, and it dilutes the existing equity. Moreover, an equity issue has to be arranged when the financial climate is most propitious, and this may entail waiting some time. Banks make long-term loans, but apart from the fact that, like all such methods of raising capital, it creates a liability, loans have to be serviced. Additionally, the company may not be able to offer adequate collateral, or it may even have such a loan already. Overdrafts are of uncertain duration.

A further method of raising funds is the liquidation of existing assets through such devices as 'sale and leaseback'. Or again, there is hire purchase and leasing which both have the advantage of making machinery and plant available to a company which cannot afford the outright purchase. But factoring combines the advantages of a number of these methods. It is a revolving, self-liquidating line of finance. Yet, it creates no liability because the funds are not borrowed, but stem from an outright sale of the book debts.

Curiously, trade debts are the Cinderella of the balance sheet, largely neglected. Yet, they present an alternative to either bank borrowing or an increase in equity or loan capital, through the more effective re-deployment of existing capital. The sum released by factoring debts is obviously dependent on the amount outstanding. Average settlement periods vary between different industries, and might range from seven days to 100 days. But typically, British companies may have 20 per cent of annual turnover outstanding in trade debts. A factor will normally advance between 70 and 80 per cent of this sum with the balance paid, minus charges, on maturity of the debts. Thus, on an annual turnover of £500,000, some £70,000 or £80,000 might be immediately released for re-deployment. If the funds are successfully used to expand turnover, larger amounts will correspondingly become available.

However, a clear cost-benefit assessment is a prerequisite, for factoring is not, by its nature, an inexpensive facility. There are two separate charges, corresponding firstly to the handling costs, and secondly to a rate of interest on the funds advanced. The first charge is a commission or administrative fee expressed in terms of a percentage of the sales volume handled under the factoring agreement. This may range from ½ per cent to 3 per cent, but is commonly between 1 and 2 per cent. It reflects the accounting administrative work and credit risks involved, and can be affected by the average face value of invoices, the number and spread of customers, the average credit periods and the element of credit risk accepted in the debts assigned. The cost of funds varies between 1½ and 4 percentage points (usually towards the lower end of the range) over the base rate of the clearing banks or the finance houses (or some other agreed barometer which reflects the current level of domestic British interest rates). If the client does not require all the factor's services, the precise charges may then be a matter for negotiation.

A direct comparison between the total cost of factoring and the price of money from other sources, is neither possible nor really appropriate. The rate of interest on funds advanced against debts would, if considered in isolation, be clearly competitive with other sources of money, probably amounting to no more than the normal overdraft rate. However, if the factor's handling commission is included in the calculation, the relative cost of this type of finance can rise sharply where no other benefits are derived. The gains from factoring have each to be considered and weighed against the expenditures and losses which might be eliminated. There are savings both tangible and intangible.

A reduction in overhead costs is the most obvious tangible saving. At the same time, trade discounts conceded by a factor's client as an inducement to his customer for early payment need no longer be offered, although there may be some customer resistance to such a

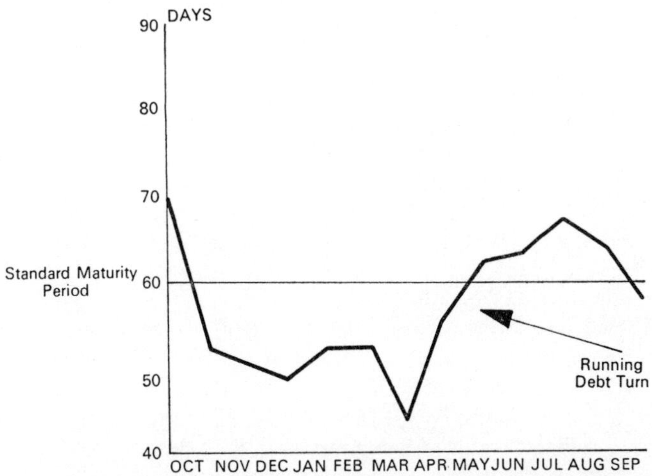

Figure 3. Debt-turn graph. This graph is similar to that used by one of the factoring houses to plot the length of time that a client's customers take to pay their trade debts. A 'standard maturity period'—the average number of days that all such debts are outstanding during the course of one year—is first established. In this example the S.M.P. is 60 days. When, during subsequent months, payments are made more quickly or more slowly, the actual running 'debt turn' rises or falls from the S.M.P.

move, while extra funds enable the client to take advantage of discounts offered by its own suppliers. For example, where a 2½ per cent discount is foregone because settlement is not made within the stipulated period of, say, 30 days, this is equivalent to borrowing at 30 per cent per annum. There can be clearly discerned savings even where the factor does not advance funds, but simply conducts the sales-accounting and collection function. A client with debts outstanding for an average of 60 days on a turnover of £500,000 has about £80,000 of capital tied up at any given moment. If the 'debt turn' can be reduced to 55 days, this will free some £7,000, and such an exercise results in no interest charges being paid to the factor.

The factor's handling commission can perhaps best be put into perspective by comparing it with the charges of other agencies offering the individual services. Thus, a computer bureau providing sales ledger accounting, sales analysis and the preparation of monthly statements, would probably charge between £1,000 and £2,500 per annum (depending on the number of transactions and the sophistication of the sales analysis) on an annual turnover of up to about £500,000.

Next, the average cost of credit insurance usually amounts to around 0·15 per cent of business covered in the domestic market and 0·25 per cent of the underwritten overseas trade. A company insuring half its £300,000 annual turnover, at the mean rate of 0·2 per cent, would pay some £300 in premiums. The extent of the cover provided ranges between 75 and 95 per cent, whereas a factor underwrites 100 per cent of 'approved' debts.

Finally, for collecting debts the more respectable agencies charge between 3½ and 5 per cent on money recovered (for debts of up to £500). But in some instances this percentage is doubled where the debts have been outstanding for more than six months.

In few cases will companies be subscribing to outside agencies for all three of these services, but the cost to them of employing their own sales ledger and collection staff, would still necessarily have to be met. So, in summary, the tangible savings that might accrue to a client as a direct result of being factored, include:

1. Elimination of trade discounts paid to customers.
2. Costs of foregoing discounts offered by its own suppliers.
3. Credit insurance premiums.
4. Outlays for credit information from specialist agencies.
5. Staff salary costs for sales ledger work (or payments to a computer bureau) book-keeping, credit investigation and control, and debt collection (or expenditure on professional collection agencies).
6. Postage, stationery and telephone outlays.
7. Legal costs and other general overheads, like office space.

In addition, the overall improvement in cashflow might allow overdrafts and other loans to be repaid, with a saving in interest and service payments. All these possible gains must be set against the factoring charge to arrive at the real net cost of the operation. At, say, 1½ per cent, the handing commission would amount to £3,000 for a client with a turnover of £200,000 per annum, or £4,500 on a turnover of £300,000 (although commission will not necessarily rise *pro-rata* with turnover). If savings were made in most of the areas where they are possible, a very considerable part if not all, of the factor's handling commission would normally be recouped.

In periods of high price inflation, the savings resulting from a factoring arrangement could be greater than is apparent from a simple consideration of the immediate gains. If costs rise, a company must either suffer an erosion of profit margins or review its pricing policy. The release of funds tied up in debts might significantly contribute to a reduction in average costs, of which expenditure associated with trade credit can often be an important component. Consequently, the price of the company's product might be held and a competitive edge won. Moreover, as will later be seen, the exporting client will enjoy a wide range of other benefits to be set against the factor's charges.

Apart from the tangible savings, there may be many less tangible advantages. These include:

1. A more efficient sales ledger operation arising from the use of specialized personnel.
2. The freeing of management from time-consuming credit problems, permitting full-time concentration on production and sales.
3. Increased opportunities to chase large sales contracts.
4. An improved credit rating because of the client's enhanced ability to make prompt payment for purchases, which often ensures supplies in times of credit shortage.
5. Generally improved competitiveness.
6. Greater potential for expansion through takeovers.

The factor has three inherent advantages in the administration of the sales ledger and the assessment of credit worthiness. Firstly, he enjoys the advantages which stem from the economies of scale, handling many times the volume of paperwork dealt with by the individual client. Secondly, the comprehensive credit files which the factor accumulates through wide experience in many fields of commercial activity, permit a rapid and continuing evaluation of credit risks. Thirdly, the factor has specialist staff, trained both to assess viability and to recognize the first emergent signs of financial weakness which might be manifested by a client's customer—known as the 'account debtor' or 'underlying debtor'.

With, perhaps, several clients selling to the same customer, the factor is in an incomparable position to observe whether that customer is purchasing more than is commercially prudent. Superimposed on to these inherent advantages are the sophisticated computer systems that the factor usually possesses, permitting detailed sales analysis.

Yet, for the prospective client the considerations do not end with the cost-benefit analysis. For if the client permits himself to become totally reliant on the factor's services, many problems may arise with the termination of an agreement. The nature of these problems will depend on the reason for bringing the relationship to an end. Normally, the agreement between the client and the factor would require several months notice of termination by either party. This would allow a phased withdrawal. In many cases the successful client will have outgrown his need for the factor's services. In these circumstances it must be assumed that the client has expanded to a size which allows the sales ledger and credit functions to be profitably handled internally. Yet, even if the client has enjoyed a spectacular success and found little further need for the financial aspects, the requirements for the factor's sales ledger accounting service may still remain.

Less satisfactorily, the factoring arrangement might be ended because the client's business is contracting. The client then has to rebuild its accounts department, hire new staff, re-establish settlement procedures and generally re-equip. A mistake in assessing the potential of a client could undoubtedly be costly. However, the experience of some successful clients which have chosen to reabsorb their own sales ledgers and credit operations suggests that the associated problems are neither a deterrent nor an insuperable obstacle. The sales ledger might confidently be expected to be in a better condition when returned to the client than when initially handed over to the factor. Furthermore, a factor will normally be prepared to help and advise a former client on the reconstruction of his accounts department for some time after the agreement has expired.

Factors and Banking

Normal banking facilities and factoring are not mutually exclusive; they are complementary rather than competitive. Indeed, as factoring has developed the commercial banks have become increasingly involved, offering factoring services as an adjunct to their other activities. The branch managers of banks may either refer potential factoring 'situations' to the bank's own factoring subsidiaries, or collaborate with independent factors who have evolved joint schemes with the banks concerned. In some instances arrangements may be tailored to involve a client's bank in the agreement.

In this way, a factor may simply be interposed between the bank and its own customer to provide a secure basis for a loan which otherwise may not be advanced. Under some such schemes, the three parties will sign an agreement under which the factor will make an initial payment of up to 80 per cent of the value of the bank customer's approved book debts. These funds will be channelled through the bank. The balance, less charges, will be released after an agreed date, also to the bank, which is in an enhanced position to advance funds to the company at its own discretion, or use the funds as an underlying security for an overdraft.

The bank has greater credit flexibility and security for its loan because the factor guarantees the creditworthiness of the ultimate debtors. He accepts the debt risk and undertakes to pay all funds or collections directly to the bank. Thus, the bank can accept potentially good clients which otherwise might have been lost to it on balance sheet considerations alone, as it is able through the factor to keep in day-to-day touch with the precise position of the guaranteed sales and collections while retaining full control of the cash inflow from them. In this way, even in times of credit stringency, the bank can help build the company into a successful enterprise. The company has access to larger sources of funds than either the bank or factor might have felt able to extend individually, and can enjoy the benefit of the factor's other services.

Such an arrangement is possible because of the conceptual differences between the operations of a factor and those of a bank. The bank lends on the creditworthiness of the client, whereas the factor is concerned with the credit standing of the client's account debtors. In the event of the factored client (the bank's customer) going into liquidation, the bank should be covered to the extent of the book debts, as they no longer rank against the insolvent estate of the client, and are therefore totally available to the bank. However, disputed debts do sometimes reduce the bank's apparent security.

Sometimes the bank is required at the outset of the factoring agreement to release to the factor any existing floating charge or debenture that relates especially to the book debts. This, it may often be prepared to do. As a result some factors find this kind of bank scheme attractive because frequently their own paramount interest is in the provision of a service to as many clients as possible. This is best achieved through the most prudent use of the factor's resources, and such schemes permit the use of outside money from the client's bankers.

Factoring and Overseas Trade

Factoring concepts assume a special pertinence in the field of international trade because of the greater commercial risks involved. Many substantial public companies, whose credit departments might be as large, or even larger, than that of the factor, nonetheless use his services because of the specialized nature of credit evaluation and debt collection in overseas countries. Several factoring houses belong to overseas factoring networks capable of providing a country-to-country operation on a global scale.

The factor's distinctive contribution to the promotion and growth of world trade lies in the popular demand to simplify settlement. Increasingly in recent years exporters and importers have eschewed the cumbersome settlement procedures inherited from less liberal times, for the simple 'open account' system common to domestic transactions. By open account settlement is meant the movement of goods independently of payment, which is then made on terms agreed between the parties, through a bank or other financial institution. It thus eliminates bills of exchange, letters of credit and documents held against payment or acceptance.

The shift to open account payment is both indicative of the renewed confidence that followed the steady reduction in post-war trade barriers and a reflection of the commercial boom that was witnessed from the beginning of the 1960s. It is estimated that at least 60 per cent of British trade with the other European Community countries is now conducted on open account terms. As much as 40 to 50 per cent of world trade may be conducted on this basis, where goods are sold on credit terms of less than six months. Amongst the members of the European Community, only in France and Belgium does the bill of exchange still play a sizeable, but diminishing, role in financing trade.

The decline in the use of bills of exchange and documentary letters of credit has reduced some of the problems involved in selling overseas. But many more, perennial, difficulties remain. Foremost amongst these is the often inordinate settlement period, which may frequently be 50 to 100 per cent longer than for comparable domestic transactions. Perhaps, 90 per cent of British exports are sold on what are notionally understood to be short credit terms. But, conventionally, this is anything up to six months. A very large proportion of the trade in this category will represent settlements made between four and six months after delivery of the goods.

Up to 40 per cent of a company's total exported turnover might be outstanding in debts (twice the average for home sales). Consequently, selling abroad can create illiquidity problems very much more serious than those caused by the provision of domestic trade credit. Unwary exporters may reach a point where they have no alternative but to curtail overseas deliveries until payments are received for earlier sales. In this event potential profit is foregone. Frequently, this problem is compounded both by a lack of verifiable information about buyers and by the resulting credit risks and collection difficulties. Equally worrying are the threat of exchange rate fluctuations, language misunderstandings, political uncertainties and the hazards of greater shipping distances.

It is in the solution of these problems that the factoring technique can be used to good effect. Open account settlement is integral to the factoring operation. In the international context factoring involves a 'package' of services capable of modification to the requirements of individual clients. Through the factor's counter-parts (or own offices) overseas, reliable credit checks can be rapidly carried out on foreign buyers, remittances speedily transferred and collections more promptly executed.

Attuned to local conditions, the factor on the spot can competently advise on marketing arrangements and distribution channels. As with domestic operations, the factor provides 100 per cent indemnity against loss through bad debts. He guarantees that payment will be made within a fixed period related to the agreed credit terms. Additionally, the factor executes the sales accounting operation, billing customers in their own currencies, and will advance funds either on the shipment of the goods, or at some later stage ahead of the 'due date'. In some cases clearance through customs will be arranged, excise duty paid, and delivery made directly to the buyer. (The factor usually sub-contracts this work out to others.) Where the shipment terms are 'free on board', the costs are, of course, for the account of the buyer and would be recovered by the factor directly from him.

Moreover, the client is usually protected against the risk of changes in exchange rates, receiving payment in sterling from the factor, who is responsible for forward currency 'cover'. Protection may also be extended against the foreign customer's failure to pay for political reasons. If a dispute arises over the goods shipped, the correspondent factor may be instructed to intervene. Problems may thus be sorted out on the spot with the minimum of difficulty, unhindered by language barriers. Written communications with the importer will also be in his language, thus helping to maintain good relations between buyer and seller. If desired, clients on sales visits abroad may receive general assistance from the correspondent factor. The foreign buyer would normally pay his local factor, who transfers the remittance to his British counter-part with the minimum of delay.

The home factor facilitating the export will usually extend funds against the outstanding debt as soon as he receives copies of the invoices, together with the Bills of Lading. Additionally, factors, in some countries, will provide pre-shipment finance, although this is advanced on a different basis and not against the security of the debts. Alternatively, the system can be adapted to enable the exporter's bank to provide all or part of the finance. A monthly account will be sent to the export client itemizing the net value of sales factored during the month, including the total amount of gross sales, the total amount of advances released, the factor's charges and the credit balance in the client's favour.

As with domestic factoring, the factor's handling commission depends on the terms of sale, the average size of the invoice, the quality of the customers' credit standing and the expected annual volume of sales. Sometimes, but not invariably, the charges for the export services will be a little dearer, as a greater amount of work is usually involved in international factoring than in the domestic operation. Fees may be apportioned between the export factor and the import factor according to the respective shares of the transactions each has undertaken. In the event of an importer not paying it is frequently his local factor who bears the loss. The interest on funds advanced will probably be at the same rate as that obtaining on similar domestic advances.

Obviously, international factoring presents a new dimension of risk for the factor, for it is not only the creditworthiness of customers and the general state of their industries that are of concern, but also the overall health of nations, particularly where there are risks of exchange rate alterations. The political and industrial troubles in Italy in 1972, for example, caused much disquiet. Whole sectors of Italian industry were unprofitable. A situation like this would probably lead to a tightening up of credit procedures, with the factor becoming more severe in granting approval for new debts incurred in a country with a very weak economy. But given a healthy political and industrial climate, the factoring technique is feasible in any country with an advanced consumer-based economy.

The Factor's Client

The number of companies factored in the United Kingdom by the end of 1972 was estimated to be about 800—only a modest proportion of the total number of small and medium-sized firms that might on any reasonable criteria represent potential factoring clients. The ideal client has an annual turnover of between £100,000 and £2M and operates in fields where the usual face value of invoices is between £30 and £400. Factoring only usually becomes an economically viable proposition where a company's turnover is above £100,000. Most factors are reluctant to accept smaller companies as clients, although there are those who specialize in such firms and will accept clients with turnovers of as little as £40,000 if they have good growth potential.

It is a maxim within the factoring industry that if a product can be picked off the shelves in Harrods it can be factored, with the one exception of livestock. This understates the versatility of the industry. Almost any company making regular deliveries, in reasonable-sized batches, on an orderly basis, can factor. The provision of regular services similarly qualifies the supplier.

For historical and economic reasons the textile industry is by far the largest factored sector, probably accounting for well over half the total clients of many factors. Light engineering is another well represented sector. But the list of industries from which clients have been drawn is long. It includes electrical component suppliers, toy, furniture and shoe makers, and manufacturers of plastics, synthetic fibres and light industrial goods. Most of consumer products can be factored.

Some service industries like office cleaning lend themselves to the factoring technique. Another area where it is frequently applied is in the provision of temporary, technically qualified labour like draughtsmen. On the Continent, factoring also extends to the professions, enveloping doctors, dentists, lawyers and architects. By contrast, the types of industries excluded because, by their nature, they present too many obstacles, tend to be those where payments are irregular, or disciplines lax, or where transactions are either very large as in the capital goods sectors, or very small as with most types of shop merchandise sold to the general public.

Factoring is often inappropriate for the building trades because many accounts can arise from the same piece of work and sub-contracting frequently gives rise to complications. Moreover, there are rarely any standard procedures, with arrangements dependent on site bargaining, an above average number of disputes over quality, and problems in collection. Factors are usually anxious to avoid transactions where there are progress payments or where there are money retentions; where they involve sales to a customer who is also a supplier to a client (except under special circumstances); and where payment is qualified (perhaps dependent on a machine working satisfactorily for a month).

Although the factor's unwillingness to operate in these areas imposes a limitation on the breadth of his activities, the majority of industries fall within his scope. A second limitation is the quality of prospective clients. A large number will be rejected either because the performance of the company is unimpressive or the management is not of the right calibre. However, this does not mean that if the prospective client is making a trading loss it will automatically be disqualified. Many firms have been nursed back to health through the services of a factor, but the capacity for recovery would have to be apparent. A change of management or a complete reappraisal of activities might be a precondition of a factoring arrangement.

The real test applied to a prospective client is whether factoring will increase its earning power. An exercise the factor might conduct would be to calculate what return the company would earn on its net worth, with and without a factoring agreement. This exercise would be most necessary when the main need of the company was an early advance of funds. Some factors apply what are known as the 'five Cs of credit'—character; capacity of management and the business; the conditions prevailing in the industry and in the economy as a whole; composition of debts; and size of capital.

If the prospective client meets these criteria, there is still a further necessary consideration. This is to establish how factoring can improve the asset-liability ratio. In factoring the client does not suffer a new liability on the balance sheet, but rather an asset reflecting the amount due from the factor. This obviously has a significant and positive effect on the current asset-liability ratio.

Liabilities		*Assets*	
Creditors	£400,000	Cash	£ 25,000
net worth	£375,000	debtors	£250,000
		stock	£500,000
	£775,000		£775,000

In the example above, the Balance Sheet shows a ratio of current assets to current liabilities of about two to one (£775,000 to £400,000). If the debts are all sold and the client receives 80 per cent of the amount of the debts (£250,000) immediately, some £200,000 would be released to reduce the accounts payable to creditors (£400,000). It may be emphasized that the client does not incur a debt for the funds received. Payment has simply been made for a purchase of debts by the factor—no borrowing is involved:

Liabilities		*Assets*	
Creditors	£200,000	Cash	£ 25,000
		balance due from factor	£ 50,000
net worth	£375,000	stock	£500,000
	£575,000		£575,000

Now, reflecting the factoring operation the Balance Sheets shows a ratio of current assets (£575,000) to current liabilities (£200,000) of nearly three to one. The operation improved the position on the Balance Sheet and consequently the client's credit standing. Clearly, the client's relationship with his bank should also improve.

Having given weight to the financial state of the client and the general nature of his industry, the factor would then finally consider the spread and character of the customers to whom the prospective client sold. A company with a concentration of business to a handful of customers presents a greater risk. On analysis, many companies which appear to have a well spread portfolio of customers, frequently in fact have two-thirds of their turnover arising from one-third of the accounts. This could result in such low credit limits being imposed by the factor on the client's sales that the arrangement would not be beneficial. But equally it could prompt a programme of prudent sales diversification.

Again, too many of the client's customers might be likely to involve the factor in unrewarding paperwork. This might make the arrangement an unattractive proposition or raise the commission charge unacceptably high. But where the customers presented both a tolerable spread of risk and paperwork, the factor's first task would be to review the settlement time taken by the client's customers and compare this with the average for the industry. If the client's credit procedures had previously been lax, a considerable tightening up might follow. Even under normal conditions debts might be outstanding on two months' deliveries. If credit taken is for 45 days and sales to a customer are running at £500 a month, a client would frequently have £1,000 owing. However, this amount would not be deemed overdue because goods invoiced in any one month would not be due for payment by the time further goods were dispatched the following month. Where payments are not made on the due date and goods are dispatched for a third or even fourth month without the first month's payment having been received, the amount owing could be substantial.

Yet, any sudden tightening up in settlement procedures would require considerable diplomacy if client-customer relations were not to be damaged. The danger of losing goodwill might be the client's first consideration. A tactful handling of the situation would probably avoid any loss of goodwill, but where a client gave greater priority to his customer relationship than to an early collection of debt, this would be respected. In this case the client would be asked to bear the credit risk involved, or part of the risk.

For the factor, one area of activity demanding considerable caution is in the manufacture of goods with a high fashion content. In an advanced, consumer-geared economy, fast changes of fashion are often the main selling point. As so many consumer products are fashion orientated, it is rather difficult for factors to avoid involvement. This shift towards greater fashion consciousness has had the effect of transforming many formerly stable industries into high-risk situations. A crucial error of judgement by a client about future fashion trends could leave it with large unsold stocks which might undermine its viability.

One such trade which has been susceptible to fashion in recent years is toy making. Where once the traditional output of dolls, teddy bears, toy soldiers and model ships contented children, the arrival of the television serial has added a new dimension. The latest game or novelty is now an overnight rage, which wanes equally rapidly—witness yo-yos, hula hoops, scoobee-doos.

The factor thus needs to exercise selectivity in his choice of client and caution in his approval of account debtors. But in normal circumstances the credit protection afforded by a factor should be total, on all approved debts. Because of the much greater spread of his risks, across thousands of customers, the factor is in a strong position to weather company failures which might jeopardize the financial position of an individual client.

Normally, a company wishing to check the creditworthiness of a buyer will have at its disposal the usual, accepted tools—trade references, bank references, credit bureau reports. It may subscribe to a credit register. But the factor has an additional, and often incomparable, credit checking mechanism. This is its accumulated portfolio of files, which are both comprehensive and readily accessible. Built on actual trading experience in many cases, they are continually up-dated with the latest available information. Yet, their confidentiality is fully preserved. This is necessary as many clients may be competing directly with each other. Although the client may not be given details about a factor's non-approval of a particular debt, it will appreciate that it was made in full knowledge of the facts.

In many ways the factor's operations are a microcosm of the national and international economies in which they are performed. Factors thus have a finger on the national pulse. The earliest indications of a shift in the financial climate will be picked up. And there can be little doubt that in recent years the financial climate has become very chilly. Rolls Royce, Lines Brothers, Handley Page, Upper Clyde Shipbuilders, Mitchell Construction and Birmingham Small Arms are just some of the companies with household names which have got into financial difficulties. The moral must be that no company, however prestigious, can be regarded as wholly safe. Credit protection is a necessary requirement of modern commerce. Britain's periodic credit squeezes, with their inevitable debt collection problems and regular crop of company failures, only underscores this point.

It is not only in times of credit stringency that the collection of debts becomes excessively burdensome. The postal strike of 1971 brought the flow of payments down to a trickle. Many companies dependent on regular receipts were sorely pressed. Rising to the occasion, several factors mounted special emergency operations across the country which succeeded in maintaining an almost uninterrupted flow of payments to their clients. There have been other examples where labour strikes have held up the payment of trade debts, sometimes because the staff responsible for making settlement have been unable to cross the picket line and enter their offices. In these conditions, the client receives payment on the due date, in the normal way, from the factor.

Perhaps, the paramount characteristic of factoring is its in-built flexibility. In spite of the often narrow confines which the advance of money and the acceptance of risk impose on its operations, the factor is able to tailor special arrangements to deal with most situations.

A Factoring Operation

An example might best serve to illustrate the nature of a factoring operation. Toymakers Henry and Alfred Hankey conduct an expanding business (let us imagine) specializing in the production of plastic model kits which are assembled and glued together after purchase. From their south-coast factory the Hankey Brothers supply direct to large toyshops throughout the home counties and the south-east of England. Their annual turnover is £500,000, and of this nearly two-thirds arises during the Christmas period. Thus, the business is geared to meeting a peak demand. By mid-November a substantial number of the seasonal deliveries will have been made and invoices sent out. A considerable sum, perhaps £300,000, could be outstanding in the form of trade debts.

However, the retailers are slow to pay. They have been stocking up heavily for the annual buying spree, and they decide to stretch their trade credit to the maximum, intending to pay after the festive holiday. But the Hankey Brothers have their wages bill to find, rent and overheads to pay and their own creditors to meet. When they receive further large orders for their products from a new department store, it is a mixed blessing rather than the triumph it should be. If they were able to collect outstanding debts the fresh orders could be met, but as it is they have already fully drawn on their overdraft. This chance to expand might have to be missed unless funds can be found to allow for the purchase of basic materials and other production expenditures.

The situation of the Hankey Brothers is not uncommon. For them a factoring arrangement could be the answer. Often, where the purchaser is a small side-street retailer, factors are reluctant to involve themselves. But, in this example, the invoice values are quite large and sales mostly to principal department stores. The Hankey Brothers are keen and competent. Henry is a good salesman and Alfred an efficient manager. The factor is impressed both with the company's books and with its operations.

The brothers and the factor decide on a trial agreement. The factor undertakes to advance a sum equivalent to 75 per cent of the face value of the trade debts—a smaller than maximum 'initial payment' to take account of the uncertainties surrounding the Christmas toy trade. If the Hankey brothers had offered goods on 'sale or return' terms, then it is unlikely that the factor would have been able to provide any money. But this was not the case and some £225,000 is advanced to help meet the new orders.

As extra funds are required to cover the seasonal peak, it is not necessary for the brothers to receive immediate payment of debts for more than two or three months of the year. However, their rented premises are insufficient for their growing needs (let us further imagine) and subsequently it is space which limits expansion. Many square feet of floor space is taken up with offices from where the accounts are administered. Initially, Henry and Alfred are chary of passing this function to the factor. They feel it is necessary for them to keep direct control of the sales ledger. Yet, there is little point in duplicating work which the factor is, necessarily, doing. In any case, they will not be out of touch with the current position because the factor will keep them fully informed with regular statements about the state of the ledger, possibly providing an aged analysis of outstanding debts.

Moreover, the factor will conduct detailed sales analysis, which could be of considerable use when planning future sales promotions. So, with the sales ledger now administered off the premises, vital office space can be converted to provide more room for production at no extra cost. This allows a parallel shift in expenditure from unprofitable clerical work to more remunerative output.

Additionally, time-consuming debts collections no longer have to be made, with all the inevitably costly telephone calls and personal visits by Henry Hankey to the accounts manager of slow-paying and unresponsive department stores. The trade credit is underwritten. So, the trial arrangement is successful, and the Hankey brothers would seem very likely to become long-standing factoring clients.

In this example, the benefits would seem clearly to have justified the costs of factoring. The handling commission over a twelve-month period would amount to £7,500 at $1\frac{1}{2}$ per cent on a turnover of £500,000. Interest on the £225,000 at, for the sake of easy illustration, 10 per cent (say, $2\frac{1}{2}$ percentage points over a clearing base rate of $7\frac{1}{2}$ per cent) would total £5,625, if needed, as in the Hankey case, for only three months. The aggregate cost would thus be £13,125. The ability of the brothers to execute their new Christmas orders would alone probably cover the factor's charges, leaving aside the other many benefits.

2 *Mechanics of Factoring*

The term 'factoring' comes from the latin verb 'facere', which means 'to make' or 'to do'—literally, one who gets things done or accomplishes things. From the same derivation come the words 'facet', 'fact' and 'facsimile'. The French have the related word 'facture', meaning bill, invoice or workmanship. In Scotland, an estates manager or bailie (bailiff) is still called a 'factor'.

For many years the term factoring has been associated in England with a type of wholesaler, particularly in the motorcar and electrical trades. Only more recently, has it been used as a generic term to describe a range of financial services linked by their common employment of trade debts as a means of liberating capital. Because of the broad use of the term, there is no satisfactory definition of factoring in its modern financial sense. This has ensured a lively controversy within the industry between the practitioners of the various methods of factoring.

It is probably true to say that there are as many operational variations as there are factoring houses. But there is one broad conceptual division within the industry; between those factors who solely provide money by discounting invoices on a one-off basis and those who purchase a company's entire turnover (except the cash trade), offering other services in addition to the provision of funds. Although the nomenclature is blurred, the former practice would not seem—judged by long-standing United States usage—to qualify unreservedly for the description 'factoring'. In America it is known, perhaps more directly, as 'receivables financing', while in Britain it has been called both 'confidential invoice factoring' and 'invoice discounting'. The last term would seem most appropriate and conventional, and hereafter will be used when referring to this kind of operation in Britain.

In the American context the term 'receivables financing' will be used.

The other (and true) form of factoring is commonly called 'old line' factoring in the U.S. and, by some curious corruption in transmission, is often referred to as 'main line factoring' in Britain. The simple term 'factoring' would seem to suffice for the purposes of this narrative.

Invoice discounting and factoring are based on the same legal precepts and involve the purchase of debts. It should be clearly established at this point that although it is conceptually convenient to refer to the factor's 'interest charge' and 'credit insurance', these terms are arguably inaccurate in a strict technical sense. As the debt is bought from the client and no lending is involved, he legally pays a discount charge, not interest. Similarly, some legal experts maintain that although the purchase of debts results in the client receiving protection against bad debts, this cannot strictly be referred to as credit insurance.

Because of the diversity within even those operations conventionally recognized as factoring, the three basic services—sales ledger administration, bad debt protection and financing—may be furnished singly or in various combinations. The first two of these three services are now normally considered to be an essential part of any factoring operation and indeed, it is usual for the sales ledger and debt protection functions to be conducted by the factor. But the one truly distinguishing characteristic of factoring—regardless of the precise services offered—is that they result from the purchase of a client's entire sales turnover.

Of the three services, it is not uncommon for the financing facility to be unused by the client, although it is always available. An arrangement which does not involve the initial provision of funds is known as 'maturity factoring'. It is normally chosen when the client is not immediately short of capital, but wishes an improved, regular and unimpeded settlement of his trade debts and freedom from credit risk. The factor will calculate the average time taken by a client's customers to settle their debts and compare this with the average 'debt turn' within the client's industry.

With the experience of its specialist staff, the good factor might confidently expect to improve on the client's existing average 'debt turn' and even surpass the average for the industry as a whole. An improvement of 15 to 20 per cent is not an uncommon achievement for a factor,

The client would then receive full payment from the factor on the average maturity date, calculated from the time each batch of invoices is dispatched. As the factor accepts the credit risk, payment is made regardless of whether the debtor has actually settled. As a consequence, the client is assured of a continuous flow of funds, enabling a better utilization of capital and greater precision in its forward planning and budgetary control.

Such 'maturity' operations account for a growing proportion of the total turnover of some factors, particularly those more service orientated. Many clients combine a basic 'maturity' arrangement with an agreement that provides for an early advance of money to be made available at short notice should it be required.

In other circumstances, it may be the factor's credit insurance service which is omitted from the arrangement. This is a less frequent occurrence. Normally a factor accepts the credit risk 'without recourse' to the client, which means that failure to recover a debt would be the factor's loss. A few practitioners, however, specialize in a type of business known as 'with recourse' factoring. Where this method of factoring is adopted, the client has no indemnity against ultimately unsettled debts. If the factor has advanced funds against a debt on which a customer subsequently defaults, the money can be reclaimed from the client.

'With recourse' arrangements are most often used by those factors who stress the financial facility above any other service. For them, this type of operation provides an extra safeguard while reducing their costs and, consequently (in theory) their charges to the client. Alternatively, where the client is selling to high-risk customers, the factor may be prepared to consider only a 'with recourse' arrangement simply because the underwriting risk is unacceptably great. Sometimes, the factor will declare that he is not prepared to insure debts from a particular customer beyond a given amount. If the client wishes to make sales to this customer which exceed this 'approved' level, disregarding the restraint imposed by the factor, then in the case of default the client bears the loss on outstanding sums above the stipulated limit.

Least common of the various forms of factoring are 'non-notification arrangements'. They are not to be confused with invoice discounting, although they share with it certain features; specifically, that the client's customers are not notified of the client's relationship with the factor, (or financing company, in the case of invoice discounting) which thus remains confidential. The practice of notifying all of the client's customers that the factor has been assigned the debts is often held to be intrinsic to factoring, but it is not universally adopted. In some cases of non-notification factoring, where even the administration of the client's sales ledger is actually excluded and where the client collects the debts himself as agent for the factor, the distinction between factoring and invoice discounting becomes very blurred indeed. But, in common with other more traditional forms of factoring, the non-notification variety involves the purchase of the client's entire turnover, except the cash transactions. This represents one key difference between factoring and invoice discounting.

A non-notification factoring arrangement generally involves the factor keeping the accounts ledger in the name of a sales company to which the client sells his debts. For example, Friar Brake and Clutch Ltd, sells its debts to Friar Brake and Clutch (Sales) Ltd. All post-delivery communications with the client's customers would then be conducted through the medium of the latter-named company. The factor would perform all his usual functions but his identity, as the true owner of the debts would never be revealed.

By contrast, the form of non-notification factoring which involved the client collecting the debts as agent for the factor (some people would question whether this really was factoring) usually occurs in exceptional circumstances, where, for example the client has only a handful of large customers. They may be large and reliable, but not necessarily prompt payers. With such a limited number of customers, the client can probably handle the sales accounting as cheaply as the factor and therefore would gain little from the factor's administration of the sales ledger.

Thus, all the various forms of factoring—'maturity', 'with recourse' and 'non-notification'—have a role to play in meeting special needs and extending the flexibility of the industry. Additionally, there are two further variations. Both are comparatively uncommon outside of the U.S., but have been modified to take account of the special characteristics of the British market and are worthy of brief description. The first is concerned with the provision of credit insurance to a client who is a substantial supplier to a handful of customers, one of whom, himself, buys only from two or three other sources. Such concentrated purchasing presents an exceptional customer credit risk and an unusual degree of mutual dependence between buyer and seller.

Under a 'special buyer' arrangement, the factor is able to offer insurance against the 'larger-buyer' risk by the use of what is known as back-to-back cover. This insurance cover is more comprehensive than that offered by other credit insurers and is effected by using the insurance principle of splitting a large individual risk over a number of separate accounts. Under this arrangement it is necessary for both the supplier and his large customer to agree to factor their debts.

The arrangement assumes that the large customer's own ultimate sales are far more diversified than those of the principal client. The ensuing 'secondary' debts created when the large customer in turn sells his wares, are then used to secure the initial credit granted by the client supplier and underwritten by the factor. Security is then achieved at one remove. If the large customer should fail to pay the client, his own debtors can be legally used as a source of funds to pay his supplier (the principal client). The factor would normally be prepared to release a limited sum, perhaps equivalent to 40 per cent of the value of the ultimate debts. This cash from the factor would be released not to the client supplier (as is the usual practice), but to his large customer (whose own debts actually form the underlying security). The balance of the 'secondary' debts are held by the factor, creating a reserve to help cover the initial credit granted. The client supplier in this way benefits from the elimination of the credit risk and his customer gains from an improved cashflow.

The second variation is called 'drop shipment' factoring and is similar to the back-to-back arrangement. The objective of this operation is to gear the client's debts directly to the payment of his own suppliers. It is primarily used in the case of middlemen, distributors or processors, where the client has insufficient capital even to purchase the goods he needs to conduct his business. A tripartite agreement is signed between the factor, the client (in this case the buyer) and his supplier. (This contrasts with the back-to-back arrangement, which involves the factor, the client and the client's customer.) But only the client is actually factored.

When the client receives an order, he immediately makes out a corresponding purchase order from his own supplier. Both are dispatched to the factor for approval. The supplier can then release materials to the client who, in due course, delivers the finished items to his own customer (the ultimate debtor). The factor will at this point make a partial payment, against this debt, to the client's supplier. Because the ultimate price of the merchandise will have been increased to allow for the client's own trading margin, the initial cash payment from the factor—of 70 or 80 per cent—might pay the supplier in full. But alternatively, the client and his supplier might share this initial cash payment proportionately. The drop-shipment arrangement is often used in international trade but can be readily adapted to domestic business. Its importance is in speeding up payment to the client's supplier while helping the client himself to build up a sufficient capital base to meet his trading volume.

Invoice Discounting

Apart from these variations on the basic factoring concept, there is, as we have seen, the related yet distinctive operation known as invoice discounting. This is frequently conducted by factoring houses in parallel to their 'main line' business, but is additionally undertaken by other specialist institutions. In one sense, banks too can be said to be regularly involved in a type of debt financing—every time they accept debts as collateral against an overdraft.

Invoice discounting differs from factoring in several crucial respects. Firstly, the financing house does not insist on receiving a client's entire turnover, discounting debts in the quantities and at the time dictated by the client (as long as the quality of the debts is acceptable). Second, an invoice discounting scheme provides no other services than the provision of finance. A client continues to adminster his own sales ledger and collect his own debts. Lastly, no credit insurance is involved as the debts are purchased 'with recourse' to the client in the event of non-payment. The client's debtors are not systematically notified of the arrangement (hence the occasional description, 'confidential invoice factoring').

At the same time, the quantative financial requirements are higher under invoice discounting than under factoring. Any one batch of invoices with an aggregate face value of less than £2,000 is unlikely to be acceptable. Only companies with a minimum turnover of £250,000 will be considered by some financing houses. In some cases the minimum figure may be even higher.

The method of charging for this facility is also different. There is just one charge, on funds advanced. This may be of the order of 1½ to 1¾ per cent per month, given prevailing bank base rates of, say, about 10 per cent per annum. When the discounting is not being used there is no charge. In many cases, where finance is required only for short periods, invoice discounting may be the cheaper of the two basic systems. But, obviously, there are none of the other benefits under invoice discounting that may be enjoyed with factoring and the objectives are of a more limited kind. The mechanisms, too, are different. Under a discounting operation the client acts as a trustee for the financing house and is responsible for seeing that customers make regular payments and for pursuing overdue debts. When customer payments are received the funds are usually lodged in a trust account controlled by the financing house. This is a necessary measure if confidentiality is to be maintained (which would not be the case if there was a simple endorsement of the customer cheques passed to the finance house by the client, unless, of course, coded endorsements were used). Customers are thus usually kept unaware of the invoice discounting arrangement.

When payments are received by the client in excess of the initial 80 per cent advanced under the discounting arrangement, they are still immediately made over to the financing house, which then makes an equivalent amount available to the client (minus interest charges). Sometimes, as collateral security for the initial advance cash payment, a client is required to accept a bill of exchange drawn on his company maturing simultaneously with the debt.

At the outset, the client lists the debts that he wishes to place in the hands of the financing house, and states the date by which it is expected that they will have been paid. Any period between 30 and 90 days is usually acceptable. When the debts have been agreed, the client sends copies of the invoices to the financing house as supporting evidence of the actual transactions.

Usually a sum equivalent to four-fifths of their face value will then be made available to the client. Each batch of debts accepted in this way by the financing house constitutes a self-liquidating, separate entity. A client may have several similar limited arrangements running concurrently.

Although, in many respects the invoice discounting and factoring systems are competitive, in practice they serve different markets and meet different needs. Some factoring houses operate both systems to provide a more comprehensive range of facilities and a greater flexibility in solving their client's problems. In some cases, where it is clear that the client requires more than just financial assistance, he might be advised to switch from invoice discounting to factoring. Alternatively, it may be thought that the client is no longer benefiting from the non-financial services of factoring and a simple cash injection, through invoice discounting, might in some cases be more suitable.

There exists also, another system of converting debts into liquid funds, an adaptation of invoice discounting. But, in this case, the financing institution becomes involved in the transaction before, rather than after the debt arises. As with invoice discounting, the client acts as an agent for the financing institution. Again, there is no sales ledger service involved and the proportion of the client's turnover covered by the arrangement is at his discretion. The arrangement is also confidential. But, this system differs from invoice discounting in two crucial respects —it is conducted on a 'without recourse' basis and, most importantly, the financing institution becomes a principal in the actual business transaction, effectively buying the product rather than the debt.

This operation does not boast its own descriptive appellation. It is usually known by the name of the single institution in the City of London which has adopted this form of financing—London Bridge Finance, a subsidiary of Hill Samuel, the merchant bank. Under the operating agreement, London Bridge becomes the 'seller', while the client adopts the role of 'agent', marketing his own manufactures on London Bridge's behalf. Buyers are unaware of the arrangement.

London Bridge accepts the credit risk. It approves customers and establishes credit limits. Every week it is advised by the client about orders taken on its behalf, whether funds are then advanced against them or not. On an agreed accounting day each week the client forwards a delivery statement and a copy of the invoices to London Bridge, which normally then pays the client their total value, minus charges. A trust account is used for customer receipts.

The charge for this facility is expressed as a discounted cash price—as London Bridge is buying and re-selling the merchandise—and is calculated by converting an annual rate of interest into a flat charge determined by the estimated average time it will take customers to pay. Only money actually received by the client in advance of the debt maturing, attracts this charge. If a customer pays more quickly than initially expected (or more slowly) the charge is adjusted.

However, London Bridge is more exposed than factors generally to the risks arising from the delivery of faulty products. As a consequence, it is rather more severe in its judgement of the permissible ratio of advances to the net worth of the client, requiring a significant margin to cover itself in the event of it taking a 'technical recourse' for the production of sub-standard goods. Such considerations are most relevant where individual invoice values are very high. An advance against a single invoice valued at, for example, £250,000, would probably be unacceptably high if the client's tangible net worth was less than about £750,000. Obviously, a more tolerant attitude is possible where invoices are valued at £250 and represent production items of 25p each.

Factoring Procedure

A factor's relationship with a client might originate at the initiative of an interested company, or follow a 'cold call' made by one of a factor's business development personnel. The involvement of the big banks also means that branch managers are increasingly watching for 'situations' amongst their local customers, on whom factoring could have a beneficial effect. Independent factors have opened provincial offices to widen their catchment areas.

A factoring agreement will not be undertaken lightly. The prospective client will first be interviewed. A preliminary inquiry into his financial position will follow, and later a more exhaustive investigation will be carried out, involving checks on plant, machinery, stocks and other assets, a thorough study of the balance sheet and an assessment of management experience and capability. This survey may be conducted by a senior factoring executive and a credit specialist. The results then might be sent to a factor's Credit Committee, or some similar body (depending on the precise procedures of the factor concerned) consisting perhaps of a chief accountant, a credit manager and two executive directors. If the prospective client is approved, the factor will quote its terms and charges, and the 'prospect' will then decide whether to go ahead with the arrangement. On a decision to do so, he signs a master agreement and the new client's sales ledger is entered into the factor's computer file.

As well as checking on the client, the factor will appraise the client's own customers—using credit agency reports (like those of Dun and Bradstreet), bank reports, trade references and information which has been officially registered. Most importantly, the factor will consult his own records. As a result the factor will be able to suggest realistic initial credit limits for each customer which will then be under continuous review. This 'discretionary credit limit', sometimes called a N.A.R.U. (standing for 'no approval required under' . . . the stipulated sum) is based on the regularity of payment and financial health of the customer.

The next stage is crucial in all standard (that is non-confidential) factoring, directing attention to the factor's claim over the debt and detailing the payment procedures of the client's customers. It involves the formal notification that the debts have been purchased. Notification letters are sent out to the customers advising them of the new regime and informing them that the assignment had been made. From that time all invoices carry a legend that might typically read:

'The amount of debt on this invoice has been absolutely assigned to (factor's name and address) who are solely entitled to receive payment. Please quote customer code number when making payment.'

A client may dispatch his invoices directly to his customer, with copies to the factor or—depending on the system practised—send them to the factor in the first instance (a relatively uncommon procedure), who then re-directs them. The latter system gives the factor a greater degree of security against client fraud. Invoices are sent to the factor in schedule form and the relevant information—client and customer codes, invoice values, dates—is fed on to the computerized ledger. This, together with credit applications and credit notes, constitutes the principal client input information and the only data prepared by him.

The only customer inputs are cheques and remittance advices. The factor's own inputs will normally consist of internally generated intelligence affecting necessary changes to the account, such as credit approvals or disapprovals, adjustments resulting from trade disputes and various other information of a technical kind.

The output documents that might be received by the client include:

1. The monthly *client statement*, detailing transactions on the customers' accounts and the client balance after allowing for funds initially advanced against the debts.

2. An *aged analysis* showing the length of time debts have been outstanding.

3. Copies of all *customer statements and reminders* sent to customers.

4. A *customer index*, giving details on a monthly basis of customers and their account numbers to help in coding invoices and credit notes

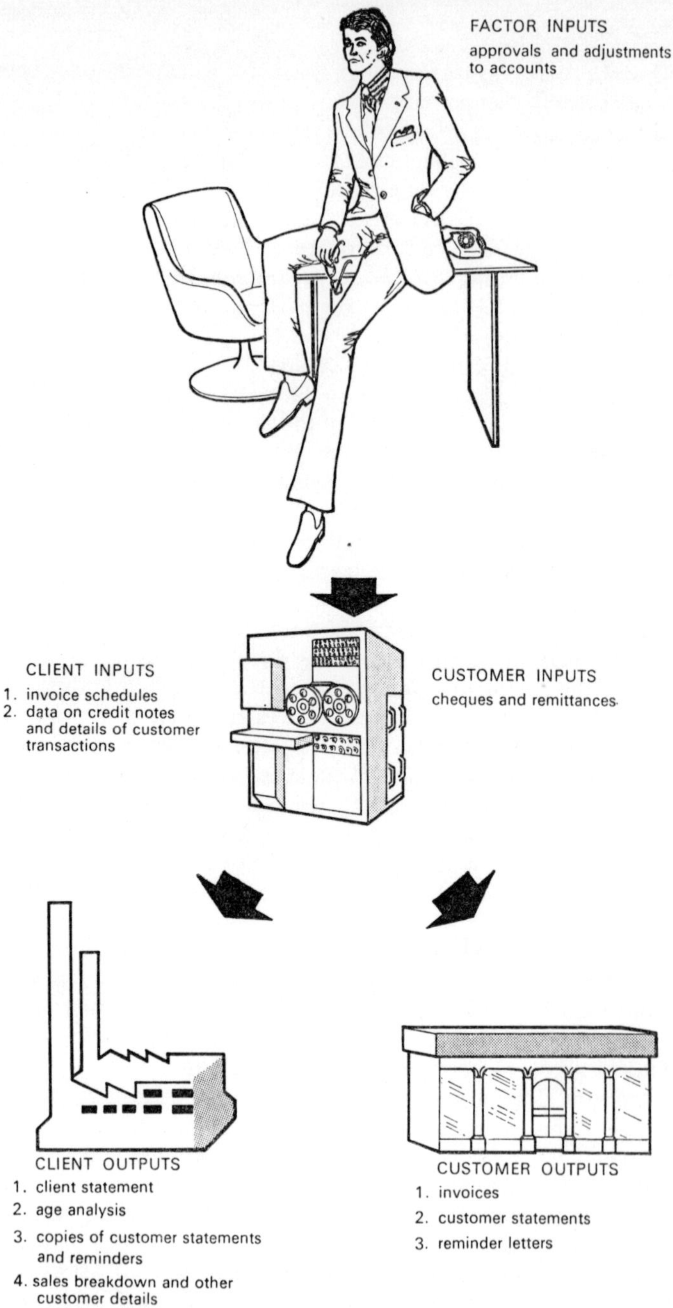

Figure 4. The paper flow.

on the schedules which the client sends to the factor; also giving details of any up-dating, revision or deletion to discretionary credit limits.

5. A *daily cash list and age analysis*, notifying the client of monies received from each customer in the previous 24 hours (this information is usual only in 'recourse' factoring).

6. A *sales breakdown*, if required, providing information on the unit sales volume analysed by customer, geographical region or salesman.

7. *Details of customers in excess of credit limit* as approved by the factor.

Precisely which material a client receives will depend on the factor's mode of operation and the client's requirements. Clients may also be furnished with copies of the factor's internal input documents which affect the accounts, and a schedule acknowledgement form giving the amount and serial numbers of schedules received by the factor. Clearly, the paper flow involved in the provision of all this data would prove onerous for the factor and unwelcome to the client if, indeed, it were all transmitted; but much is dispensed with. The factor's charges, outlined on the monthly client statement, are automatically debited to the client's account.

The documents that the customer might receive from the factor are far fewer in number and include:

1. Top copies of *invoices and credit notes* (where the invoices are not sent directly by the client).

2. Monthly *customer statements*.

3. *Reminder letters*, usually first sent when the debt reaches maturity.

Organizational Structure

The organizational structure of a factoring house is normally divided into four distinctive parts—accounts, customer credit, collection and clients (*see* Fig. 5). The servicing of the debtor's accounts (handled in the department on the extreme left of the organizational chart) is, in many ways, central to the whole operation. Debtor accounts are constantly needed to enable the factor to perform the credit insurance functions. These accounts register the development of the security for the advances to clients. Here, too, the client's sales cashflow is monitored, together with the input of invoices and the receipt of payments.

One of two methods might be used by this department for maintaining the sales ledger, One is the 'balancing method', whereby customer transactions are recorded in chronological order, with balances

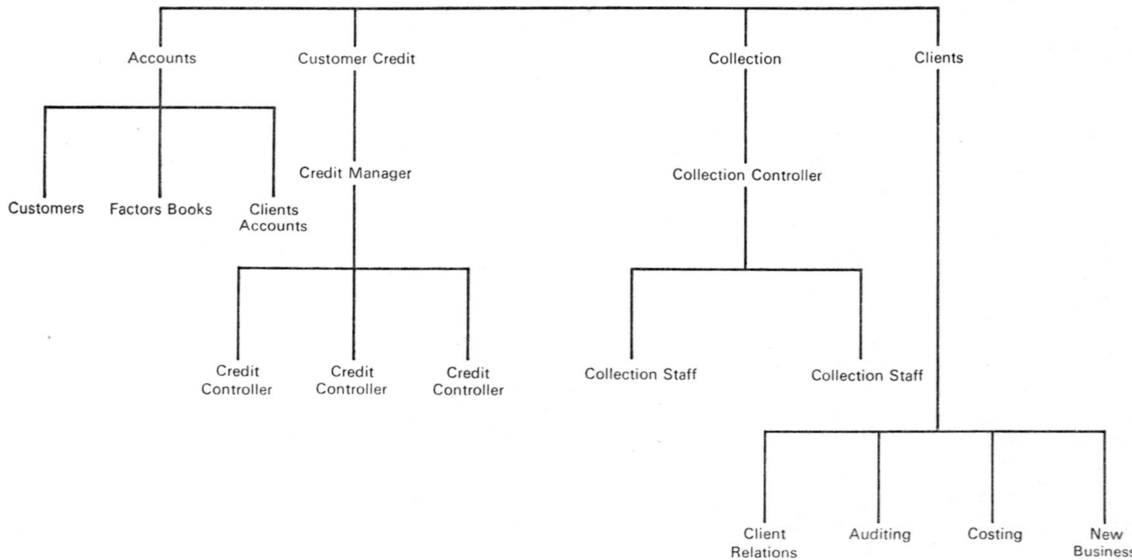

Figure 5. Organization chart.

struck and carried forward at regular intervals. The second method is the 'open item system'. Under this system a balance is struck after each transaction is recorded. As cash received is matched against specific invoices, it is always possible to reconcile the open items on a sales ledger card to the balance outstanding. This allows those invoices which are outstanding for payment at any one time to be identified and highlights the period of credit taken.

The factor's own accounts, its profit and loss account, depreciation, and staff costs, may be handled within the same division.

The clients' accounts section can be viewed as the banking department, making advances to clients and constantly checking the volume of these advances against the debtor balances. Indeed, some factors allocate the client two accounts; one logging the advances made and the other recording the debts purchased. As one is credited the other is debited. For example, under a maturity' arrangement, with debts outstanding for an average 60 days, the client's 'advances account' would be credited on the 'due date' and the 'debts purchased' account would be debited by a similar amount. In this way a strict relationship is maintained between advances and the debts upon which they are made.

The next principal division is that of debtor control, where the credit insurance underwriting is conducted. This is where requests for credit approvals are made, appraised and accepted or refused. The amounts that a credit controller can sanction depend on his experience and seniority. The credit manager would be authorized to approve credit limits of several thousand pounds. Larger sums might have to be passed up to the general manager for approval. But, even those credit requests requiring deliberation and investigation would normally receive a decision within 24 hours.

The watchword for the division responsible for collections must be diplomacy. Collections are a sensitive matter and the client is often chiefly concerned about his relationship with the customer. Procedures for dealing with bad payers are well defined. Quick identification of slow payers and early action by the factor's collection department can often result not only in prompter settlement but in a better understanding being established with the debtor. For some large commercial companies it is a management policy to keep suppliers waiting for payment as long as possible. Large electronics companies, particularly, have a reputation for delaying payment. The factor's collection staff are fully aware of the delaying tactics employed, and have techniques for countering them.

Suppliers are naturally hesitant to serve a writ on a large customer as legal proceedings are tedious and often embarrassing. This is a weakness that some customers are prepared to exploit, particularly in times of tight national credit policy and high interest rates. They stretch out their payments to less important suppliers. The factor's routine collection procedure will require that customer statements be rendered as soon as possible after the close of each month, detailing goods invoiced up to the end of the month, but normally requiring payment a month hence.

A second statement will be rendered a few days beyond this due date. If payment is not made fairly smartly after maturity of the debt, a reminder will usually follow around the middle of the succeeding week and a further statement will be dispatched when the debt is about five weeks overdue. The debtor may receive anything up to four or five letters graded in severity of their wording. Usually, they will be personally signed by a senior manager or director.

Before this stage is reached, any accounts that the debtor has with other clients will receive scrutiny, further deliveries will probably be curtailed, his credit standing will be reviewed and the factor's other departments will be alerted to the situation. As well as sending letters, considerable use will also be made of the telephone in an attempt to contact senior personnel within the debtor's payments department. Resort may, in addition, be made to registered letters and telex messages. If none of this succeeds in prompting payment a final strongly worded letter may then be sent, informing the debtor that legal proceedings are being instigated for non-payment of debt. Only the insolvent or the most recalcitrant of debtors permits the collection process to pass beyond this point.

It usually requires a policy decision by the factor's directors to put legal wheels in motion, placing the matter either in the hands of an independent firm of solicitors or the factor's own legal representative.

Ideally, the client will have been consulted at an early stage in the collection process, but permission would certainly be sought before any legal action were embarked upon. To protect themselves, some factors might feel compelled to sue the debtor even against the client's wishes, where the unpaid debt amounts to over 50 per cent of all debts purchased from that particular client. However, many factors will not override the client in such matters, although the client would, in such circumstances, have to be prepared to assume the risk and suffer the loss if no payment was ultimately forthcoming.

If the client concurs with the factor's action, then no question of any such eleventh-hour assumption of risk by the client arises. Where the sums owed amount to a sizable percentage of the client's turnover, the factor may choose to enforce his rights in spite of opposition from the client, to protect himself and any bank partner involved. In any case legal proceedings are a last resort only. The threat of legal action alone usually leads to a settlement of the overdue account. Generalizing, perhaps around 0·4 to 0·5 per cent of factored turnover is the subject of legal representations, and in the experience of some factors, only between 0·05 and 0·1 per cent is ultimately unrecoverable.

A good many unpaid debts result from misunderstandings or technical difficulties and precipitate action by the factor to collect in these circumstances could result in the loss of much goodwill. For example a customer may not have paid because he is waiting for a screw for a recently purchased machine tool. The failure of the customer to inform the factor of this situation can pose considerable difficulties. Contra payments and credit notes also require speedy adjustment to the account if a reliable debt profile of the customer is to be maintained.

A trade dispute between client and customer could also be an explanation of non-settlement. A dispute might arise because the client supplied the wrong quality or quantity of goods or because certain specifications have not been met. In these circumstances the factor would send a Notice of Dispute to the client. A copy would also be sent to the collection department to forestall any precipitate action. The established disputes procedure would then be followed. The client may—if he has clearly not adequately fulfilled an agreement—then be given a month to rectify the situation. If the dispute is not settled satisfactorily, the disputed item is debited to the client's reserve, and an adjustment is made to the next advance to restore the reserve to the required level. For the factor, keeping the ledger 'clean' is an overriding objective.

After the accounts, customer credit and collection divisions, on the organization chart comes the division concerned with client relations. As most of the larger losses suffered by the factors in recent years have resulted from weaknesses within the client, this last division assumes no less importance than the others. With good credit control, most factoring houses have succeeded in keeping down their bad debt losses to acceptable levels, but eliminating losses resulting from clients' failures can prove more troublesome.

Factors, therefore, like to keep the financial position of the client under close observation, watching the development and direction of his business and the quality of the underlying debts—as opposed simply to the promptness of the debt settlement. Any deterioration in the quality of the debts (greater incidence of credit notes) needs to be detected at an early stage. The factor makes regular visits to the premises of a client, the frequency depending on the factor's view of the strength—or weakness—of his financial position. An obviously sound client will be visited every three months perhaps, but one facing difficulties may be seen at more frequent intervals. Again, in the former of these cases, the factor may be satisfied with just the company's annual report, while in the latter, much more detailed figures will be required.

Much of the factor's client division is concerned with new clients: marketing, costing the new 'prospect' to permit a quotation, and auditing (effectively a survey rather than a full-scale audit). But, these departments also conduct re-costing operations on established clients —illuminating for example a drop in average invoice values and permitting an increase in commission—and, of course, re-auditing. Finally, there is a department concerned with the smooth conduct of client-factor relations, ironing out problems, attending to client grievances, and gathering and collating information to secure the safety of the factor's advances. This latter function constitutes a cross-check on the client's position and has proved very valuable.

Failures, Frauds and the Case of the Disappearing Pig

The factor's protective mechanisms for safeguarding against client fallibility or delinquency are comprehensive and elaborate but not impregnable. The factor is particularly vulnerable to deliberate fraud, and the ever-present possibility of chicanery is an accepted hazard. If advances are made against falsified invoices—for example where several sets of invoices are dispatched against a single order of goods, or perhaps, where invoices are composed for non-existent customers— the factor, of course, has no security. There were at least 8 to 10 frauds in the industry between 1964 and 1969.

But it is not only fraud that has to be guarded against. In some cases, client negligence can result in the factor making unjustified payments. insufficient liason between the client's dispatching and invoicing departments may mean that the factor is sent invoices for merchandise which has been held up in the warehouse. Again, the failure to disclose the provision of credit notes, issued, perhaps, only after a considerable delay, could lead to greater sums being advanced than are warranted. Or the factor's position might be undermined as a result of customer retentions or counter-claims, disputes over quality, or because further work is necessary before payment can be enforced.

But the biggest single threat that the factor faces remains the claiming of funds under false pretences. To this end, it is not unknown for client and customer to conspire together. The danger of paying other than legitimate debts might be lessened by the factor taking a charge on the client's stock or other assets. But this is not usual, partly because these assets are often already the subject of a charge held by a bank.

Apart from routine checks and the alertness of his personnel, the factor's main protection against systematic abuse is the 20–30 per cent retention (or reserve) on all debts. In the early days of modern factoring in Britain it was common practice to advance funds to the equivalent of 100 per cent of the face value of the debts. But this practice was quickly found to leave the factor dangerously exposed and the system was refined to allow the advance payment of 70–80 per cent of the debts and the creation of an effective reserve, although even this is not a very effective safeguard as the reserve is paid out on the average maturity date.

There are a few precautions that the factor can take in establishing that he is purchasing only bona fide debts. He can insist that all the client's invoices are, in the first instance, routed through him, as opposed to his receiving only copies. A programme of verification is also followed. This entails obtaining confirmation of customer balances by circularizing customers on a random basis. The verification is carried out with the client's knowledge but not his participation. During the periodic visits to the client's premises by the factor's personnel, particular attention will be paid to the client's routines and general method of operation, to ensure that there are no inherent weaknesses which might affect the factor's security.

Few factoring houses have escaped losses arising from deception or carelessness by clients, and substantial sums have been lost by factors whose procedures proved insufficiently stringent to detect unsatisfactory situations at an early stage. As a consequence, more rigorous procedures have been steadily adopted in an effort to combine a speedy and simple system with protection of the security.

During the past decade, in at least one case, losses were suffered by a factor on such a scale that they probably came close to threatening its ability to continue in existence. The factoring house in question, International Factors, Britain's oldest and largest, saw virtually its entire capital of £500,000 wiped out early in its history.

One United States factoring house, Mills Factors, was financially broken, having lost a sum estimated at $20 million. However, in this case, it would seem to have been due to miscalculations on Mills' receivables financing activities (similar to British invoice discounting) that the money was lost, rather than as the result of defective procedures on the actual factoring business. Even so, it gives a stark indication of the kind of potential large-scale losses which could be suffered by the unwitting.

It is perhaps significant that while the amount of bad debt losses suffered by the British factoring industry during its brief history is probably between £1 million and £2 million (calculated at 0·05 to 0·1 per cent of turnover, which is the generally accepted 'norm') total operational losses, including client write-offs, are estimated to have exceeded £6 million.

Industrial and gem diamonds, sausages and farm machinery are amongst the products which have been at the centre of celebrated and instructive factoring episodes. The case of the Royal Victoria Sausage Company looms large amongst these, for it represents part of a financial deception which stretched out to encompass Her Majesty's Government and the Royal Bank of Scotland, resulting in their joint loss of over £1 million. The business of the Royal Victoria Sausage Company was the packing of bacon and other meats and their distribution to schools and hospitals throughout the south east of England.

The company's title was claimed by its moving spirit, a Mr Dennis Lorraine, to stem from a special recipe for sausages graciously commended by Queen Victoria, although in reality it was taken from the name of the road in which the company's premises were located. An interest in the rearing of pigs and micro-wave oven cooking offered the opportunity of a complete vertical operation, extending through the curing and preparation of bacon to its ready-cooked delivery.

For International Factors, however, it also provided the chance to lose a lot of money. At the peak of their relationship something of the order of £120,000 was outstanding to International Factors on debts invoiced by Royal Victoria and against which funds had been advanced. Some £50,000 alone was ostensibly outstanding on an account for Smedleys. But as events unrolled it became clear that goods to the value of £60,000–£70,000 had not even been delivered. This was explained as a clerical error and, under strong pressure from International Factors, the unmerited advances were repaid.

The money for this purpose, however, would seem to have been part of development funds for an enterprise at Glenrothes, north of Dundee, in which both the Government and the Royal Bank of Scotland had invested heavily. In fact, on investigation, the visionary Glenrothes pig-farm scheme was shown to exist in little more than name, and a Receiver was appointed. But, for once, the factor did not lose his money.

It was about this time, the mid-1960s—when International Factors lost almost all its capital—that a very different situation arose to confront this same factoring house, in an affair involving gem diamonds. Centred on a jeweller importing raw materials from Israel for the manufacture of rings, this episode provides an unmistakable lesson of the disservice that factors can do their clients through over generous credit policies. Successive increases in the credit limits which International Factors permitted the jeweller's customers, brought the total outstanding to well in excess of £90,000 and appear to have enabled him to overtrade seriously.

The unconventional nature of this particular situation was vividly illustrated by the lodging with the factor of eight boxes of emerald rock as collateral. This material, pledged by the jeweller at £35,000, proved, when the financial storm broke, to be of considerably less immediate worth because of the distinction between its value as a raw commodity and its ultimate yield when converted into finished articles. As a consequence the jeweller could only be prevailed upon to re-purchase it—in part payment for his debts—at some £17,000.

A more bizarre twist to these events occurred when, at the peak of the jeweller's problems, a valuable package of diamonds was allegedly stolen from his car. The ensuing £40,000 legal battle between his creditors and Lloyds underwriters was lost by the former group on a technicality.

The bitter experiences suffered by International Factors in the diamond trade were compounded by another, and potentially much more costly, episode, when a client dealing in industrial diamonds ambitiously sought to undercut the market. He lost the game when the market unaccountably moved against him. Only a debenture, prudently taken by International Factors, enabled the latter to limit its losses to about half the £200,000 which it had at risk. Of such events as these were the formative years of British factors made, contributing to the evolution of the procedures and operational systems practised today.

The largest single client loss involved a company called Spiraflite, which collapsed in November 1971. At that time some £866,000 was reported to be outstanding to H. & H. Factors. Spiraflite represents the most spectacular and classic factoring loss so far. The company marketed a kind of corkscrew elevator for raising corn up to lofts. It also manufactured silos and the machines which made the elevators.

H. & H. Factors advanced funds, it seems, against invoices for goods which were not dispatched from the Spiraflite warehouse. These particular undispatched items were warehoused together with other, identical goods not yet earmarked for any buyer. As a consequence, H. & H. Factors had great difficulty in identifying and proving title to 'their' goods in the warehouse, against competing claims from other creditors. Two Spiraflite directors owed a total £4 million, representing one of the largest individual failures since the war, according to the Official Receiver.

But, as the greater U.S. factoring experience shows, effective procedures and diligent cross-checking can only limit such losses, not eliminate them. The practice in America for factors to conduct stock financing in addition to purchasing debts, has widened their area of risk and has been the stimulus for ingenious fraudulent schemes. The common aim of most of these schemes is to create the impression that more stock or finished manufactures exists than actually is the case, thereby beguiling the factor into advancing more funds than justified.

In one celebrated case, metal tanks made by a client and housed in his factory compound, were revolved on large swivels so that the same items were unwittingly counted more than once by the factor's personnel. In another case, vats of liquor were furnished with false bottoms to give the impression that they contained larger quantities than they actually did. The moral for the factor—one that has been taken to heart—is that effective and competent procedures are the fulcrum of the operation, and need continual refinement.

3 A History of Factoring

'Percy is but my factor, good my Lord,
To engross up glorious deeds on my behalf;
And I will call him to so strict account
That he shall render every glory up,
Yea, even the slightest worship of his time,
Or I will tear the reckoning from his heart.'

1 *Henry IV*, Act 3, Scene 2

'The said William Eyrus was factor, not only for His Grace the Duke of Norfolk, but for many others, worshipful merchants of London.'

Richard Hakluyt, *The Great Voyageur*

'Nay, on my life, it is my factor's hand . . . I'll think on the account.'

Christopher Marlowe, *The Jew of Malta*, Act 1

'Factors are in the trading world what ambassadors are in the politic world.'

Joseph Addison, in his *Royal Exchange*

Factoring, in some form, dates back to antiquity. A factor was a key figure in the economy of the Roman empire. Wealthy senators and nobles entrusted the management of their property and their agricultural produce—corn, wool, oil—to agents who received a commission for their services. This agent was often called a factor. Sometimes he would be responsible for finding buyers for the produce of the large estates, which often entailed making long sea journeys. In such cases, he might pay the nobleman in advance. The Phoenicians, another mercantile people, also adopted such methods of trading.

Roman factors were, themselves, often rich—and sometimes unpopular—men. Claudius, the Roman Emperor forced a number of corn factors to help finance his scheme for converting Ostia into a safe winter harbour. This scheme he hoped would eliminate the danger of corn famine, as the corn could be more easily shipped from Egypt and Africa. It seems that the factors were not well disposed towards this idea as it reduced their grip on the trade. Yet Claudius, it appears, obliged them to finance the harbour to the extent of 1,000,000 gold pieces.

The commission-agent form of factoring was recorded again in the 13th century. By the beginning of the 14th century it was widely conducted in North Italy. Where the commission agent sold on credit, he probably also took the credit risk as otherwise he might have been tempted to extend over-generous terms to buyers that were poor credit risks. The principal would quite likely have lived in a different town to the agent-cum-factor, perhaps even in another country. It would thus be impossible for him to appraise credit risks.

Later the term 'del credere' appeared. This was a term borrowed from Lombardian acceptance bankers; the factor would stand 'del credere'. In 1771 a Swedish economist, Johan Hartman Eberhardt, defined the term in the following manner: 'del credere is the undertaking on the part of a commission agent to assume responsibility for the credit-worthiness of the buyer or his ability to liquidate his debt on the due date'.

For this assumption of the credit risk, the agent would be compensated by a special 'del credere' commission. There is a clear parallel with modern 'maturity' factoring. Factors placed in differeet markets to buy and sell goods on commission contributed substantially to the expansion of trade which developed from the early 16th century. Factors followed the Portuguese out to the East Indies. The foreign trade of flourishing towns like Milan, Genoa, Lyons, Madrid and Barcelona depended heavily on the services of factors acquainted with local markets, who bought and sold on a commission basis. They accounted for much of the world trade in raw materials such as wool, indigo, hemp, cotton, iron, sugar, corn, rum and tobacco.

From as early as the 14th century the factor had also become an important influence in the textile industry—an industry which was to play a fundamental role in modern day factoring. Sometime later, Blackwell Hall became used exclusively for the transactions of business by factors and their clients—mostly in textiles. As trade blossomed the English Government became eager to capture new markets and did much to encourage textile manufacture. This brought forth heavy demands for textile goods and the factor was similarly encouraged to help manufacturers meet increasing demand. Thus there arose, particularly in and around London, a large and important class of textile factor whose business was to sell and finance the rapidly growing commerce in silk and wool.

The East India Company then took over a great deal of the import and export shipping. It became necessary for the company to have a responsible agent-factor at each of the colonial trade posts. His duties appear to have included making advances on silk, wool and other commodities. So by this time a financing element had clearly become integral to his services. Apart from advancing funds, the factor attended to shipping documents and generally performed many of the functions familiar to factoring today.

During the 16th and 17th centuries the so-called 'factorage system' was almost universal in Europe. This system involved the granting of long term loans or the proffering of advance payments to manufacturers, who only in this way could acquire funds for raw materials, fuel, wages, warehousing and transportation of goods.

The marketing of the goods was often conducted by the agent who granted the loan. 'Bottomry' was a form of credit granted by a commission agent at the time of the loading on board of the merchandise and the credit was secured by pledging both cargo and vessel. Bottomry also functioned as marine insurance since, in the event of the loss of the ship, the borrower was not obliged to repay. Because of the slow movement of goods in these days, bottomry loans also functioned as a form of warehouse financing.

During the 17th and 18th centuries the Netherlands was financing a large part of the world's commerce and production, and the Dutch came to be described by Montesquieu and Voltaire as the 'factors of the whole world'. Historical records show that in France and Germany during the 1850s advances were being made directly against 'receivables' (the outstanding debts on goods delivered). This was also practised in Austria during the 1890s. In Vienna, advances against receivables seem to have been commonplace up until the First World War.

In Germany the procedure of granting advances against receivables was stopped by a decree issued by the Reichsbank in 1911. This had repercussions in other countries, and in Sweden the Bankers Association decided not to include advances against receivables among the services offered by member banks. Operational problems of ledger accounting and collection contributed to this decision. Meanwhile, factoring in the form it had this far developed, became a backwater in Europe. The great merchant houses and trading houses had moved to the centre of the stage by the peak of the colonial era.

However, their operations were not unakin to those of the factor that preceded them. It is no coincidence that many of the confirming houses have in recent years played a major part in the reintroduction of factoring into Britain. But until this development, the term factoring had come to be associated, since before the First World War, with a kind of wholesaler, particularly in the electrical, metal hardware and motor-car fields. By contrast, in the United States between the wars, factoring, which had been taken across the Atlantic by the early settlers, was receiving a new lease of life.

Factoring goes West with the Pilgrim Fathers

It must be stressed that the type of factoring that began to flourish in America in the 1930s bears only a sketchy resemblance to that taken westwards by the Pilgrims. Within half-a-dozen years of the Mayflower leaving Plymouth in 1620, a number of settlers formed a general partnership on behalf of the entire colony, to trade colonial and English merchandise. This was done in an effort to earn sufficient money to pay off the debts incurred in financing their venture.

One of the colonists returned to London and concluded a deal with three of the financiers, under which they agreed to become partners in the trading arrangement. These three were to purchase merchandise in England for the account of the group—shoes, cotton and woollen cloth, linens, bed-ticks, blankets, salt, spikes, nails, tools, pistols, muskets and powder and shot—which would then be sold by the settler partners to other settlers, or traded with the Indians and the European fishermen on their annual voyages to the fishing banks off Newfoundland and Nova Scotia.

The London partners would, in turn, receive and sell on the settlers' behalf, all the shipments from the colony, primarily beaver, bear, mink, fox and otter furs, fish and timbers. Unfortunately, this trading agreement did not turn out as planned. The records were poorly and incompletely kept both by the London partners and the colonists, making a reconciliation of accounts increasingly difficult.

In the trading agreement, the London partners were termed 'agents and factors'. Throughout the colonial era from this time onwards, the term 'factor' was used to describe an intimate, personal agent who took care of the local financial interests of one of several distant business enterprises. He was really a merchant who performed a wide variety of supplementary specialized services. A British factor, for example, was the principal correspondent of one or several colonial business merchants or firms. He sold on a commission basis the products of the new land; tobacco, furs, skins, fish, lumber and lumber products, which the colonial exporter shipped to him. He also sold the colonial trader merchandise out of his own stock, at the current prices, when they were wanted.

Merchandise which the colonial importer ordered, but which the British factor did not carry, would be purchased for him from other British merchants on a commission basis. The factor arranged insurance on his customer's ships and cargoes, forwarded letters, made payments on his behalf, and advanced funds, when necessary, at the usual rate of interest, providing the colonist's credit was good. All the large ports, Bristol, Liverpool and London boasted several factoring houses.

Several British merchants, in turn, kept factors in the colonies and on the islands of the West Indies. In this case, the factor in the overseas outpost was an employee sent from the home office. He kept a stock of consigned merchandise for his employer, developed sales, and acted as financial agent and confidential adviser on the extension of credit and on the outlook and problems of the colonists. As settlements were made and expanded, trade developed.

By the second quarter of the 19th century, the business of the factor in America had evolved into that of a distributor of merchandise, largely for the European manufacturers and exporters on a commission basis. The other services which he had earlier performed had receded to minor importance. He customarily received a commission of about 5 per cent on the value of the foreign products which he sold, and 2½ per cent on domestic products. The terms 'factor' and 'commission agent' had by this time become quite synonymous, although the factor was probably more representative of the firm that handled the imported merchandise. Goods would generally be sold on credit terms.

But as the country was opened up and settlers moved west there was naturally a growing insistence by manufacturers for some form of payment guarantee before they would allow blankets, cloth and other goods to be dispatched into often hostile territory. To this extent the manufacturers on the Eastern seaboard of America were at just as large a disadvantage as the Lancashire and Yorkshire mill owners. The factor would guarantee that the sales made on credit would be paid on maturity of the debt. For this they would receive a further commission of 2½ per cent.

If collections were made, still a further 2½ per cent would be charged. When it was necessary to engage in litigation, a commission of 5 per cent was added. For purchasing, remitting or collecting bills of exchange, the factor usually received 1 per cent, and for drawing, endorsing, accepting or selling drafts or bills of exchange, the figure was again 2½ per cent.

Equally significant by this time, was the commission agent's function of advancing funds, usually up to two-thirds or three-quarters of the market value of the merchandise, to those for whom he was selling. Credit terms were seldom less than 30 days and usually 90 or 120 days in the textile industry. Commission agents became an important source of finance.

In the first 40 years of the 19th century, the population of America more than trebled, to 17 million. Textiles of all kinds were in great demand for wearing apparel, bedding and furnishings. Many of the commission agents which originally imported merchandise on their own account, gradually began to handle more consigned merchandise from the European textile mills. They took charge of the goods from these mills, which they often directly represented, found buyers, guaranteed their customers' credit, made advances generally once a month against these receivables, and made additional advances against the consigned merchandise. They thereby provided the mill with continuity of operation and ample working capital to buy materials and pay its labour.

The commission agent played a tremendously important part in the growth of America's fabric industries. The value of textiles manufactured rose from $36 million in 1860 to $207 million in 1870, the wartime boom stimulating production and purchasing power. Wool mills sprang up not only throughout the New England states, but in the Philadelphia district as well. During 1862, no less than 115 new factories were built, nearly all producing woollen goods.

Around the turn of the 20th century the commission agent-factoring business underwent a radical change, The selling function was gradually discontinued and the factor essentially became a specialized banking type of institution for the textile industry.

This represented an important development in the evolution of the factor from the commission agent of previous centuries to the institution of today. One of the first factors to move in this direction was Oelbermann, Dommerich & Company, operating in New York City. It had represented many European mills and by 1889 handled an annual volume of sales amounting to some $15 million.

Emil Oelbermann resided in Cologne and handled the European end of the business, while Louis F. Dommerich managed the New York office. For the latter, this meant supervising the sales in the U.S. of a wide variety of textile products, keeping in touch with markets, styles and prices and advising the European manufacturers on how best to accommodate local demand.

The workload became so heavy that selling merchandise on a commission basis was discontinued. With the elimination of the selling function, the factor became a specialized banker. He continued to perform all the other services. Before an order for merchandise was filled, the order would be turned over to the factor who would decide if the buyer was financially creditworthy. If he was, the factor would guarantee the payment of that account to the mill making the sale, and at monthly intervals would buy these receivables outright from the mill without recourse. Advances would also be made against stocks of merchandise.

There was another element in this evolutionary step. Towards the close of the 19th century, shifting population centres, and a marked speeding up of the pace of deliveries because of improved transportation, wrought changes in distribution. Manufacturers frequently found it more convenient to ship direct from the mill, rather than send goods *en bloc* to the commission merchant.

Various devices were resorted to, in an effort to preserve the 'factor's lien' while goods remained under the manufacturer's own roof. Sometimes a separate space was partitioned off in the mill's warehouse and a custodian was appointed, bonded by the factor to have charge of the goods stored within the enclosure. Or again, a warehouse might be rented, either in the mill's own town or at a convenient nearby 'shipping point' (which, in American usage, included inland as well as seaboard points of dispatch). In either case, there was a conspicuously posted notice to the effect that the goods were 'under lien'. A lien is defined as a right in law to retain the property of another to pay a claim.

But in spite of the problems thrown up by the changing conditions, the greater convenience and economy of shipping direct to customers was leading the mills in this direction, no matter how much they might value the credit and financing services of the commission merchant. An increasing number of mills began to sell their own output either directly to retailers or through distributors.

Thus a type of account was presented to the commission merchant in which he was called upon to do no selling, but to advance money against the debts resulting from the sale, while still, in most cases, undertaking to guarantee the solvency of the buyer. A different mode of procedure was adopted from that which had existed when the commission merchant had actually sold and shipped the goods. The mill's name now appeared as the seller on the invoice, and for the protection of the erstwhile commission merchant a notice was stamped or printed on the face of the invoice, stating that:

> This account is assigned to,
> owned by and payable only to (name of commission agent)
> New York, N.Y.,
> in New York funds

However the name 'commission agent' was now no longer appropriate, for he was no longer selling goods on commission. Meanwhile, the word 'factor' had largely fallen into disuse, being limited to certain buyers of raw materials, principally cotton and wool. The word lay slumbering in the lawbooks, where its meaning was well defined by the courts and the rights which it implied were fully guaranteed by decision and statute. So before the turn of the century, Charles Evans Hughes, then a rising lawyer and the attorney to a famous commission agent called James Talcott (later a famous name in factoring) drew forth the word 'factor' from its legal limbo.

The McKinley tariff of 1890 completed the evolution from commission agent to factor. This tariff repealed the duty on raw sugar, and reduced the duty on steel rails, iron and steel plates. It also raised duties on woollen cloth and the finer grades of cotton, lawns, embroideries, linens and plush goods. The general level of all duties was increased to an average of 49·5 per cent. In the case of textile products, these duties now became almost prohibitive.

Overnight the business of the then commission agent dropped off as prices of European textile merchandise, with the added duty, became too high to sell in the American market. The only solution was to concentrate on domestic business. Those commission agents which hitherto had represented foreign mills turned their attention in this direction.

But with most American mills now preferring to run their own sales departments, the selling end of the commission agent's business was by this time drying up. Thus, the factor came into being with three distinctive functions: he assessed the creditworthiness of customers from whom orders had been received and in most cases he cashed the sales—that is bought these receivables outright without recourse: he made cash advances to textile mills, selling agents, and converters against finished merchandise as security; and in some cases he performed a group of special services such as providing space for display and storage of merchandise, handling insurance, billing, packaging, shipping and making city deliveries.

From around 1890 to 1930, factors did business primarily with those textile mills, selling agents and converters that sold their products to the clothing manufacturers, department stores and—as they developed—the chain stores. Throughout this period, factoring remained highly specialized, showing no tendency to expand into fields other than textiles. However, some factors did begin to gather some peripheral accounts in new fields. These accounts were in the main for manufacturers of men's, women's and children's haberdashery such as kid gloves, handkerchiefs, scarves, infants' wear and specialities, and some piece goods.

The annual volume of these kinds of items sold on factored accounts to retail trades other than department and chain stores (that is women's speciality stores, remnant and drygoods stores and men's clothing and haberdashery stores) was very nominal compared with the volume of piece goods sold to the cutting-up trades and larger stores—probably a small fraction of one per cent of total goods factored.

But small incursions into non-traditional fields continued into the late 1920s, receiving considerable stimulus following the stock market crash of 1929 and the Great Depression when the textile trade shrank, along with the factors' profits. The recovery in the American economy found the factoring industry operating on a much broader base, handling much more varied lines and, consequently, in a much stronger position

By the early 1950s ,when the re-birth of factoring as a major force in commerce really began, the portfolio of accounts had been widened to include manufacturers and traders in cosmetics, chemicals, fluorescent products, yarns, furniture, portable organs, garden hose and nylon fishing lines, as well as companies in the metallurgical industries and wholesalers of glasswear, gloves, hosiery, radios and electrial appliances. Shortly, factoring began to attract the attention of the banks, heralding a further stage in its development.

The Arrival of Receivables Financing

At this point, it is necessary to chart the course of a parallel industry which had grown up in the first half of the 20th century. In 1904, the first 'accounts receivables' finance company was formed in Chicago, making loans on assigned accounts. This activity was what came to be known as 'receivables financing' (invoice discounting in Britain). It began when an enterprising encyclopedia salesman found himself short of cash. Since he was selling his books on instalment credit, he found his receivables mounting rapidly as his sales increased.

An account receivable (or simply, a receivable) is the American term for an ordinary trade debt. Thus, the textbook definition of an account receivable is an 'open-account indebtedness arising from the sale of goods or the rendering of services'. If the seller does not receive payment on delivery and if he does not retain a security interest in the goods sold, through perhaps a conditional-sale contract, his right to receive payment for the goods is an account receivable.

As the encyclopedia salesman had exhausted all his available sources of credit, he sought a lender who would advance cash against his receivables. He found such a person and they became partners, quickly recognizing the value to business of this type of operation. They intended, in fact, to operate in the same manner as factors by having the account debtor (the client's customer) pay the financing company directly. But this met with resistance from potential clients who feared that the necessary notification to the customer of the receivables sale, would result in suspicion being aroused about their financial strength. Although factoring was widely accepted in the textile industry, there was little comprehension of it beyond this field. This contributed in large measure to the difficulties faced by factors when they initially attempted to widen their horizons.

At this time, however, factoring had not begun to extend more than timidly outside the textile industry. As a result, the two partners worked out and applied a different system. This was to have the client assign the receivables to them, but make the collection himself in the normal way. This system allowed the arrangement to be kept confidential. The client was designated the agent of the finance company and was obliged to commit to it all collections. Advances against receivables were made on a 'with recourse' basis so that any bad debt losses were borne by the client. Some funds were also retained as a reserve.

After nine months of operations had proved that the venture was both practical and profitable, the business was incorporated by the partners, John Little, the erstwhile encyclopedia salesman, and Arthur Jones, as the Mercantile Credit Company of Chicago. The demand for their type of financing grew and the number of finance companies supplying this service increased markedly. Slowly, an industry began to take shape, developing a detailed operating matrix, which is used today. Duplicate invoices were required, together with evidence of the delivery of the merchandise, independent verification of the account with the debtor, periodic audit of the assignor's books, original cheques, or other form of settlement, and a copy of the debtor's payment statements.

During the Depression, a few banks began to operate in the receivables financing field, but they did so primarily to gain security over loans which had been made originally on an unsecured basis to companies subsequently finding themselves in financial difficulties. As a result of this tendency, receivables financing came to be associated by many banks with corporate weakness. As a consequence they largely remained aloof from this type of operation, leaving it to specialist finance companies.

As what became known as the 'commercial finance' companies flourished they developed additional techniques for providing funds, notably by means of liens on equipment and inventories. By 1920 there were 100 small and medium-sized finance companies in the field. In spite of the industry's considerable growth, it did not really become a major economic force until after the Second World War.

The volume of business transacted by American commercial finance companies in 1941 was about $536M. Only 15 years later, it totalled over $5,500M, some ten times greater. By 1960, there were over 800 commercial finance companies listed (against some 50 factors). Turnover reached $16,250M by 1965 and almost $22,000M by 1970. This compares with factoring, which was by this time a good deal smaller at nearly $12,000M.

Receivables financing has, in its comparatively short history, been responsible for nurturing numerous clients which have later achieved national prominence. Two companies with household names—Dow Chemical and Monsanto Chemical—were amongst the earliest to adopt this method of raising funds. Other companies have benefited and grown to become leaders in their industries, including National Airlines, Continental Motors, Diner's Club, Lithium Corporation, Helene Curtis, and the Jim Walters Corporation.

4 The Legal Framework

At the heart of a factoring arrangement is the master agreement, which forms the basis of the factor-client relationship and establishes the manner of the operation to be undertaken. The purchase of book-debts is accomplished by means of an assignment. But the precise legal position of the factor and his title to the security are ambiguous in many countries including Britain. In America, the development of factoring has rested on a composite foundation: a cautiously conceived modus operandi, an elaborate contractual framework, common law principles and specific legislative enactments. In recent years, the adoption of the Uniform Commercial Code, almost throughout the United States, has provided a much more consistent and systematic basis for all secured transactions than existed there hitherto. In Britain, the legal position of modern factoring is unclear. No single law specifically governs the factoring operation: rather it has been devised (or improvized) to fit between existing laws like the Money Lenders Act, without infringing them.

The principal legal theme throughout the development of factoring has been, not surprisingly, the need to establish beyond doubt a title either to the goods against which money was lent (this was the case during earlier years), or to the debts purchased. In early English and American factoring, where merchandise was physically handled by the factor, the main desire was to effect a 'lien' on the goods. (A lien is a right to retain the property of another in payment of a claim.) But, as the selling function was reduced and the purchase of debts became predominant, an enforceable assignment became the primary legal objective.

For the commercial finance company, which conducts non-notification receivables financing in the U.S., the lien (still usually referred to as the factor's lien) remains important. This is because this type of financing differs in a practical sense from factoring, and until recent years was legally distinct from it. Whereas, under factoring, there is an *outright sale* of the accounts receivable (the debts) the other form of financing involves, in America, the assignment of the receivables by the client to the financer *as collateral for a loan*. In addition, of course, the commercial finance company does not assume the credit risk, does not usually require that the account debtors (the client's customers) be notified of the assignment and does not collect the accounts. His prime function is as a provider of funds.

This fine distinction between transferring accounts by way of an *outright sale*, and by way of *security for an obligation*, resulted in separate legal consideration during the inter-war years. The question of a lien does not arise from an outright sale of an account receivable, for there is nothing on which to take a lien. After the factor's metamorphosis, his residual interest in the lien only surfaced in situations where there were inventory loans or, perhaps, where merchandise had been returned by the account debtor and not yet re-purchased by the client.

Thus, while the assignment of receivables as collateral for a loan required that a lien be perfected on the collateral, (perfection being necessary in case there was a second lien on the same collateral), the notification legend on invoices was sufficient in most instances to perfect the factor's title to the accounts before the Uniform Commercial Code was adopted widely. In most states the legal significance of such notice was well settled. Although since the adoption of the Uniform Commercial Code it has been made legally redundant, the practice is still widespread. It meant that where an account debtor, who had been notified, paid his supplier instead of the factor, he could be liable to pay again to the factor. In addition to the legal reason for notification, there were (and are) strong operational reasons for this system. It gives the factor greater control over settlement monies and establishes lines of direct communication between factor and account debtor.

To appreciate further the legal position of factoring it is again necessary to trace its genesis. In Britain there were two almost conflicting, prevailing attitudes towards the factor in the 16th and 17th centuries. The first was the official attitude, which was to encourage the factor in the interests of trade. The second was the widely-held belief that as middlemen, factors were in some way parasitical. One person who wrote as long ago as 1692 concerning Blackwell Hall factors maintained that: 'Here are a considerable Party of Men that flourish like Solomon's lillies, that neither toyle nor spin, that only get a profit out of the Wool, and no way encourage the Woollen-Manufacture.'

The writer's preoccupation appears to have been with the hardcase of the manufacturer in the 'clutches' of the factor. The outcry against the English textile factor in the 17th century resulted in an Act of Parliament. The case against the factor was that he had been selling on unduly long credit terms, that he had been slow in remitting to the clothier, and, in some cases had even used these remittance monies to buy wool to sell to the clothier at a profit.

It was also alleged that many factors used these and other means to ruin the manufacturer, and so acquire his business. The Act, passed in 1695, proved very severe. It required the factor to be licensed, limited strictly the credit terms on which credit sales could be made, provided for periodical reports of sales and goods on hand, and insisted upon prompt remittances. However, the Act quickly proved out of keeping with the rapidly changing times. It shortly became a dead letter. Factors were able to circumvent it; both by dealing with the poorer merchant, promising them prompt sales and, in the case of sales on credit, by guaranteeing the account himself, for a commission.

Far more important to the development of early factoring was a judgement some 50 years later in the Chancery Court, made by Lord Hardwicke. In the 15th and 16th centuries, the factor did not receive title to the goods, although he was nevertheless responsible for their safekeeping as well as for the proceeds which were received for the sale. The Chancery Court case was concerned not with textiles but with logwood brought to England by ship. The judgement helped to establish the factor's lien, based on possession. In a far-reaching pronouncement, the court ruled that a factor to whom a balance was due, had a lien upon all goods of his principal, so long as they remained in his possession. As the manufacturer was, in this particular case, bankrupt, the court was initially inclined to the accepted canon of equality for creditors. But the opinion of merchant witnesses giving evidence on 'custom and usage', was sympathetic to the factor—a man called Mico. Although Mico the factor actually lost the case because he had turned over the goods to his principal's broker, the merchants agreed that where there was a general account between factor and principal, the factor might retain both ship and cargo not only for particular charges but for any balance due to him on the general account. This judgement was enormously important in helping to establish the factor's lien.

Later, the lien was even extended to include 'a lien on the price of goods in the hands of the buyer,' (as well as ship and cargo). Although the factor did not in this case have 'actual possession' of the goods, 'yet as he had a power of giving a discharge, or bringing an action, he had a right to retain the money' paid to him by the buyer.

The courts were sympathetic, in the main, to the commercial classes and eager to give them support in the struggle for supremacy over the other great European states. They hoped that a general lien would encourage factors to advance cash upon goods in their possession and speed up the circulation of money—the lifeblood of trade.

A number of general Court case rulings which appeared to undermine the factor's position—like the one in 1743, which held that a factor could not 'affect the property' in his principal's goods 'by pledging them as security for his own debt'—were simply reversed by the first Factors Act, of 1823. The general effect of this Act was to define by statute the Common Law relationship between factor and principal, for the protection of both, as well as third parties. Meanwhile, the factor's lien, his security in the goods on which he advanced money, seems to have been transmitted to the U.S. as a matter of course. In 1830, the New York legislature confirmed the existence of the lien by statute.

By the later 19th century, with factoring in Europe a spent force, the focus was on developments in the New World. In Britain, the second Factors Act, of 1889, was to be of little material significance in the general context of the continuing evolution of factoring. Indeed, this Act was intended to govern the sale and purchase of goods conducted by a species of trader akin to a wholesaler—in fact, the atavistic and atrophied descendant of the factor who 50 years earlier had played such an important role in European commerce.

But, in the U.S., where factoring had remained a more dynamic force and where the factors were providing increasingly more finance to the textile mills, they were demanding greater security than just the goods in their possession. They required liens upon other of the mills' assets, including raw materials, goods in process, and finished goods in the possession of the mills themselves. As the role of the factor changed and the selling function was dropped, the courts came increasingly to question his general lien, based as it was on possession. For he rarely now ever actually took delivery of any of the mills' goods, as the mill was often selling directly by this time to wholesalers and retailers. Moreover, he was beginning to be seen as more of a commercial banker than a factor, in the conventional definition employed by the Courts. Frequently, factors resorted, during the transitional period, to the expedient of setting aside those goods upon which money had actually been advanced, in a separate part of the millowner's premises, and posting a sign over them clearly stating that they were the factor's property. In this way factors hoped to preserve their title on goods financed but no longer physically handled. Gradually, new operational procedures were evolved. The practice was set and consistently followed that the client-manufacturer made an outright 'sale' of the accounts receivable to the factor, customers being notified that debt payment should be made to the factor. Additionally, it was established that merchandise disputes between client and customer were the supplier's responsibility, the latter agreeing in all factoring arrangements to indemnify the factor against losses arising from such disputes.

But the operational changes raised for the factor a fresh legal issue to supersede his previous preoccupation with his lien on goods. It concerned the actual transfer of the assignment. For the sale of an abstract item like an 'accounts receivable' arising from the sale of goods, evoked difficult points of law in the same way as the factor's lien had done in earlier times. The receivables finance company, also gradually developing at this time, faced in many U.S. states particular difficulties in perfecting a lien on accounts receivable taken as collateral for loans. Yet perfection was imperative for the security of the lending company. In both English and American law a debt, or account receivable, falls within the general category of a 'chose in action.' This is a right of proceeding in a court of law to procure the payment of a sum of money, e.g. a debt, a bill of exchange, policy of insurance, or an annuity. This right is conferred, for example, on a manufacturer when he sells on credit. In early English law it was originally held that choses in action were not assignable. But this early rule was later circumvented by the use of powers of attorney. The power of attorney has enabled the assignee or attorney to sue in the name of the assignor and to keep for himself whatever funds he collected as attorney.

In America, the precise requirements for establishing a valid assignment differed greatly between the states until the 1950s when the Uniform Commercial Code began to be adopted. Previously, factoring and receivables financing were governed by a variety of differing state laws. Indeed, the problems posed by such differences had an important influence on the basic operational matrix that evolved for these forms of financing.

Under both factoring and non-notification receivables financing it is essential that the rights in the accounts transferred to a factor or financer be valid as against a liquidator, receiver or trustee in bankruptcy of the assignor (the client).

Similarly, the assignee's (the financer, whether factor or finance Company) rights need to be protected against a subsequent attaching creditor or a competing assignee. Where such competing assignees are in evidence, they usually indicate dishonesty by the client, attempting to obtain double financing.

It became well established in United States law that an account debtor was not prejudiced by an assignment of which he had no notice. While notice to the account debtor was not essential to the validity of an assignment between a client and his financer, until such notice had been given the account debtor could continue to regard the assignor (the client) as the owner of the account, making payment to him. If the debtor was subsequently sued by the assignee (the financer) he could assert this discharge of the debt as a valid defence. On the other hand, if notice of an assignment was given to the account debtor (as it was, and usually still is, in factoring) this notice was binding upon him and he was obliged to pay the assignee. If instead he paid the factor's client after such notice, this was not usually recognized as an effective discharge of the debt.

The laws governing factoring and non-notification receivables financing before the adoption of the Uniform Commercial Code fell basically into three categories. These were the so-called English Rule, American Rule and Massachusetts Rule. In most states it was accepted that an assignment of an account without notice to the account debtor was fully *effective* against a judgement creditor or an attaching creditor or garnishee of the assignor. But there was no similar uniformity or certainty as to whether an assignee of a chose in action prevailed over *another assignee whose assignment was later in time* but who first gave notice of assignment to the account debtor.

On this point the leading English case of *Dearle* v. *Hall* was the origin of the old common-law rule known as the English Rule. Under this it was held that the assignment became effective upon the account debtor *being notified* of the transaction. And, in the event of two assignments of the same receivable, the *first assignee to notify prevailed.* From eight to fifteen states followed this rule.

But a majority of states followed the indigenous New York or American Rule which maintained that *priority in the date of assignment* rather than *priority in the date of notification* to the account debtor, determined rank between successive assignees of an account receivable, or chose in action. This rule of course most readily accommodated the type of non-notification operation conducted by the commercial finance companies.

The intermediate Massachusetts Rule (adopted by only two states) stated that an assignment without notification was effective unless a second assignee had collected the account in good faith, reduced his claim to judgement, obtained a novation, or secured evidence in the debt in the form of an instrument.

Because it became established practice in factoring to inform the account debtor of the arrangement there was little difficulty under any of these rules in perfecting assignment. However, where the account debtor was not notified and the possibility existed, as under the English and Massachusetts Rules, of a second and superior assignment arising, considerable difficulties were created. This posed a serious problem where receivables financing was conducted. And the whole situation was made even more difficult in 1938 when an amendment was passed to Section 60 of the Bankruptcy Act. This amendment concerned the giving of 'preferences'—the transferring of assets to a favoured creditor within a short period before declaring bankruptcy. The particular amendment stated that certain transfers made by a bankrupt within four months preceding adjudication of bankruptcy were 'preferences' and *were voidable by the bankrupt's trustee in bankruptcy*.

The specific clause of the amendment that left the commercial finance company vulnerable was one concerning perfection of assignment. This asserted, in effect, that where an assignment had not been *perfected* prior to bankruptcy it would be deemed to have been made immediately before bankruptcy. As, under the English and Massachusetts Rules there always remained the *theoretical possibility* of either a subsequent attachment by a creditor or subsequent assignment, the non-notification assignments were thus, for the purposes of the bankruptcy court, *not perfected* if the subsequent attaching creditor or assignee could acquire rights superior to the actual assignee.

As a consequence of this, the effective date of the assignment could be postponed to the date of bankruptcy, declared to be in breach of the provisions on 'preferences' and set aside by the trustee. The threat this constituted to non-notification receivables financing was soon recognized and by 1954 a total of thirty-six states had enacted special legislation to remove the risks created by the 1938 amendment. One way round the problem chosen by fifteen states was the enactment of so-called 'validation' statutes, which provided, in effect, that accounts receivables assigned for value in good faith and in writing were valid when made, whether or not notification was given to the account debtor.

Meanwhile, in nineteen states statutes were enacted providing that assignments of accounts were valid provided that public notice of the accounts receivable financing was given by some form of public notice or filing. Two states idiosyncratically passed statutes providing that assignments of accounts receivable were valid as long as the books and records of the assignor-client were marked to indicate the assignments. With the changes in the law undertaken by these states and the continued observance by several states of the American Rule that assignments were valid when made, without regard to notification, the position of the finance companies engaged in non-notification receivables financing was protected and their ability to perfect a lien on the collateral much extended.

Factoring under the Uniform Commercial Code

The year 1954 was an important milestone in the legal development of factoring in the U.S. That date marked the first state enactment, by

Pennsylvania, of the Uniform Commercial Code, which has become the dominant legal influence in the field since, subsequently emulated by almost every other American state. In fact, because the Federal union is a group of sovereign states there had been increasing diversity in commercial law by the turn of the last century which had been causing a chaotic situation as interstate trade and commerce continued to mushroom.

This gave rise to the desire for uniform laws. In many fields uniform laws were enacted in the opening years of the century. However, it was not until the early 1940s that the American Law Institute started the Uniform Commercial Code project. The U.C.C. finally went into effect in New York in 1964. The Code itself deals with commercial law generally, but Article 9 deals with secured transactions specifically, removing procedural differences, unifying nomenclature, establishing the universal filing of public notices and detailing the manner of perfecting a security interest.

The Code says that a factor to whom accounts have been sold is a 'secured party' with rights similar to the holder of a lien, in fact like the receivables finance company. Thus factoring and non-notification receivables financing are placed on a similar footing. The reason for this is that the basic elements of the financing operation are identical whether accounts are transferred by way of a security for an obligation or by way of an outright sale. The underlying function of the transaction is considered of primary importance, even though the forms of the two transactions differed under traditional legal concepts. Under Article 9, an 'account' is defined as 'any right to payment for goods sold or leased or for services rendered which is not evidenced by an instrument or chattel paper'. The financer of accounts receivable is included in the term 'secured party', which definition specifically refers to both a lender and a person to whom accounts are sold.

A 'security interest' is defined as an interest in personal property which secures payment or performance of an obligation and includes the interest of a buyer of accounts. 'Collateral', under the Code provisions, is asserted to mean the property subject to a security interest and includes accounts which have been sold. Most importantly, the Code declares that a security agreement is effective according to its terms between the parties, against purchasers of the collateral and against creditors of the client.

The security interest is perfected, whether arising from an outright sale or the assignment of receivables as collateral for a loan, when (*a*) the financer and his client sign a security agreement spelling out the terms of their arrangement and (*b*) a simple financing statement is filed giving public notice of financing. Proper filing under the U.C.C. gives the financer protection against the client's creditors in case of his bankruptcy. The filing is very simple, doing nothing more than giving notice to the world at large that a particular financer is engaged in financing the accounts receivable of a particular producer, and describing any collateral. It does not require that the world be told the value of the accounts, the interest charged, or any other financial details. The filing fee is just a few dollars. A single filing is usually enough, in the state or jurisdiction where the assignor-client keeps the records of the accounts in question. Occasionally a second filing is required by some states if the place where the assignor keeps his books is different from that of the first filing.

There is no change under the U.C.C. in the account debtor's obligation to pay the factor; if he pays the client, the factor may force him to pay again. In addition, the factor has a recorded lien against any merchandise which is unaccepted, rejected or returned by the buyer. So merchandise will not, therefore, fall into the bankruptcy estate available to creditors at large.

The Law in Britain

In Britain there is nothing like the Uniform Commercial Code to help the factor through the legal shoals. He has to steer his way around a number of Acts, including the Law of Property Act, the Stamp Act, the Money Lenders Act, the Sale of Goods Act and various Companies Acts. And this leaves aside the European Communities Act. Most factors have regular recourse to counsel and few would welcome a definitive test case in the courts at the present time. However, with a few notable exceptions, most of the basic legal principles which have governed American factors, are also common to Britain.

Probably, the most important single difference is the practice in Britain of raising stamp duties on a wide variety of documents. The Stamp Duty Act of 1891 is the basis of the present law on the subject. If this law were applied to the assignment of debts, it would require payment of duties amounting in recent years to 1 or 2 per cent of their value. This could render factoring impractical as the duties would increase the cost of his services to an unacceptable level or eliminate his profit. However, a method of operation has been devised which permits debts to be assigned without incurring stamp duty.

This is achieved by taking an equitable assignment rather than a legal assignment. The assignment of a 'chose in action' can be either equitable or legal but the former represents only general acceptance of the transaction and, in the eyes of the law, is not completed until a stamped document exists establishing ultimate title to the debts (which is the case in legal assignments). As a consequence, generally the factor takes a Power of Attorney which permits him to execute a legal assignment in favour of himself in the event of his having to take court proceedings in his own name against a debtor.

Some factors believe it is possible to avoid stamp duty without using the device of an equitable assignment. Instead, they seek to take advantage of an exemption in the Stamp Act which permits, without the payment of duty, any assignment valued at under £10,000 . . . providing there is certificate of value that it does not form part of a larger transaction or series of transactions. Whether factoring forms such a continuing transaction is a fine legal point. Where the £10,000 exemption has been exploited, legal experts have advised that each schedule of invoices forms a separate legal assignment, while the master agreement simply constitutes the foundation for the trading arrangement. In contrast, under an equitable assignment the master agreement itself forms the underlying basis for transferring beneficial ownership of the debts. The statute governing matters relating to assignments remains the Law of Property Act 1925 which permits wide interpretation in this area.

Unlike the situation in the U.S. case law in Britain would seem to suggest that there is no legal difference between factoring and invoice discounting (receivables financing). Both appear to constitute an outright sale of debt.

Notification is actually required only for a legal assignment (and thus, where an equitable assignment has been used, it is strictly necessary only before court proceedings take place). Even so, as noted in the American context, notification is of considerable operational convenience. It helps to ensure that payments are made to the factor and not to the client, giving the factor greater security, although the customer would not as a result seem to be under any obligation to make payment to the factor rather than his supplier.

Under an invoice discounting arrangement, the financer does not, of course actually collect the debts, and retains an agreed right of recourse to the client. In addition, in spite of the declared confidentiality of the arrangement, the financer would, in the event of his client's bankruptcy, normally take a legal assignment and notify customers. For factors, a further precaution is open: obtaining from the client a warranty to cover delivery and quality of goods.

Two other points also arise in any consideration of the legal environment in which the British factor operates. The first concerns the factored client who already has normal bank financing. English banks commonly secure their loans to corporate borrowers with a floating charge over all the assets, including book debts and other 'chose in action'. Such a charge would prejudice the factor's title to the purchased book debts and a formal release of the debts from this charge has to be negotiated with the bank. However, the bank's charge will then, following agreement, embrace the single book debt due from the factor to his client; and of course where the factoring arrangement is without recourse, the banks' security will be stronger over that single debt than it was before over the aggregate of its customer's *uninsured* receivables.

The second point is that there is no provision for public notice of factoring arrangements and it is thus impossible to establish if the prospective client is already factored. A search at Companies House will reveal a charge, but will not show whether there has been a previous assignment of the debts and this has presented a major problem to the factoring industry.

Factoring and the Crowther Report

The Committee on Consumer Credit, headed by the late Lord Crowther, made some recommendations in its report, published in March 1971, which, if enacted, could help provide the factor with a more clearly defined legal position. However, it was felt by many practitioners that even the Crowther Committee, for all its experience, had not appreciated the conceptual distinctiveness of factoring. Consequently, a memorandum, signed by most members of the industry, was sent to the Department of Trade and Industry, setting out their position in regard to the Crowther Report. The memorandum supported the Committee's proposal for the public registration of security interests. This proposal would mean, if it became law, that a factor could readily establish whether there were any existing security interest in a prospective client's debts.

A further gain under the Crowther Committee proposals would be the safeguarding of the factor's position after the registration of an interest—title going to, and remaining with, the first to register. At the moment, the notification to the account debtor of the assignment demonstrates the factor's title, but it is not secure where, for instance, the client sells the debt twice—the first to notify does not acquire title. However, where the debtor makes payment as directed by the initial notification, this amounts to an effective discharge of the debt, if he does so bona fide, even if there is a second and stronger title to the debt.

More broadly, the Crowther Committee recommended the wholesale scrapping of Britain's antiquated credit laws, notably the Moneylenders Act, Bills of Sale Acts, the Pawnbrokers Acts and Hire Purchase Acts. These would all be repealed. In their place a Lending and Security Act would be created (and also, although not germane to the present subject, consumer protection legislation introduced). Whether the Government ultimately accepted and executed the recommendations, the factoring industry considered it prudent at that time to have its position fully understood and on record so that its interests were not overlooked in the framing of any legislation. The industry went on, in its memorandum, to suggest that the *ad valorem* stamp duty be abolished on assignment documents. This would bring to an end the clumsy system of equitable assignments.

Many of the factoring industry's suggestions were adopted from the Uniform Commercial Code which it took as its model. Clearly, if the Government were to enact a law based on the Crowther Committee's recommendations it would constitute the legal framework for many years to come. Therefore the industry was keen not only that factoring be acknowledged in its own right as a financing and service facility, but that it should be permitted to develop its potential fully.

In the absence of an early Government initiative, some British factoring houses attempted to establish their own central registry. This was to operate independently of the participating houses, but allow checks to be carried out on prospective clients for existing assignments. However, this project failed ever to become an effective industry-wide affair. The registration of clients, it was felt by many factors, represented a breach of confidentiality. If it were law, registration with the proper authorities would be a fact of commercial life, about which all would be aware. As it was, the existence of the factors' registry would not usually have been disclosed to the client. The general distaste and, perhaps, the impracticability of the register, caused most factors to continue to rely for their protection on the thorough financial checks and audits in which they were practised.

National Laws and the Multinational Factor

In many other countries besides America and Britain, the emergent factoring industry has had to accommodate local laws and commercial customs. This has particularly posed problems for the multinational factors. In Continental Europe, a series of obstacles have been encountered which were not faced in the Anglo-Saxon countries, although the sympathy of some national administrations, and a growing body of case law, have helped many of these difficulties to be overcome.

For the multinational factor, permission usually had to be obtained from central banks or finance ministries when either taking a stake in a nationally constituted company or transferring the necessary funds from abroad or raising the capital locally.

An almost universal question that has arisen is whether the factor must conduct his business through a bank or other type of financial institution, or through an ordinary corporation. In West Germany, institutions other than banks could purchase invoices without prior government accreditation, but they were not able initially (this rule has now been modified) to lend funds against invoices. On the other hand, in Italy, factoring could only be conducted through ordinary companies.

The assignment of invoices in Belgium operates only in favour of banks and officially recognized financial establishments. Therefore, factors are obliged to qualify as such establishments before the competent national credit supervision authorities. This is similar to the situation prevailing in France. Factors there have turned to the concept of subrogation (the substitution of one party for another as creditor) in order to circumvent the inherent legal difficulties. This means that contemporaneously with the advance of funds to an account opened in the seller's favour on the books of the factor, the seller gives him a subrogation release. Once the buyer has been instructed to pay the factor by a notice on the invoice, the latter's right against a third party are established as effectively as those of his American counterpart. This approach has been successfully tested in several courts, one case surviving a challenge before the Court of Appeals of Paris.

The companies Act of Victoria, Australia, requires that notice of intention to assign debts be filed fourteen days before assignment is effective. During the interval before effectiveness is achieved, creditors of the assignor may apply to prevent assignment. If each assignor (client) were required to comply with these procedures with respect to each buyer, the volume of paperwork would tend to impede the flow of purchased accounts necessary for a successful factoring operation.

Obviously, in international factoring the wide divergence of law and procedure can make export-import factoring rather more precarious then domestic factoring in, say, Britain.

Fortunately, establishing precisely which national legal system applies in the event of a dispute occurring during an international transaction, is less difficult than might be supposed. The factor is normally secure if he and his client are within one jurisdiction, as generally will be the case. As a matter of practice, the factor must then collect according to the law recognized by the debtor. For the debtor to question the factor's title—as opposed to raising a merchandise dispute—is virtually without precedent.

5 Trade Credit and Shrinking Liquidity

There has been little investigation into the magnitude of trade credit, but undoubtedly it is of a very large order. At times of severe national credit restraint the figure probably rises substantially. Trade Indemnity, the principal domestic credit insurance company in Britain, estimates that at the end of 1970, the volume of trade debts amounted to some £18,000M. This represented a rise of 20 per cent in just two years. The significance of the figure can be judged by comparing it with bank lending. At the end of 1970, the value of trade credit was some 2·8 times greater than the total advances of all the banks in great Britain to the manufacturing, construction and service industries, plus agriculture.

Evidence compiled by the old Board of Trade—which received information regularly from several hundred companies—suggests that the level of outstanding trade credit rose steadily throughout the 1960s, in line with the growth in bank lending, climbing rapidly during the difficult 'squeeze' years that followed the devaluation of sterling in 1967 (*see* Fig. 6). However, in spite of this expansion in trade credit, it grew less quickly than bank lending. As a consequence, the ratio of trade to bank credit revealed in the accounts of companies reporting to the Board of Trade, appears to have fallen from almost 6:1 to nearly 2·8:1 (*see* Fig. 7).

That the volume of trade credit rises appreciably during times of national credit stringency is a not surprising, but nonetheless disquieting, fact of commercial life. It is not surprising because, clearly, at such times company liquidity is being strained and the inclination to take increased credit is greater. But, for the creditor, it is likely to be disquieting because these economic pressures may very probably result in an increasing number of bankruptcies and financial loss.

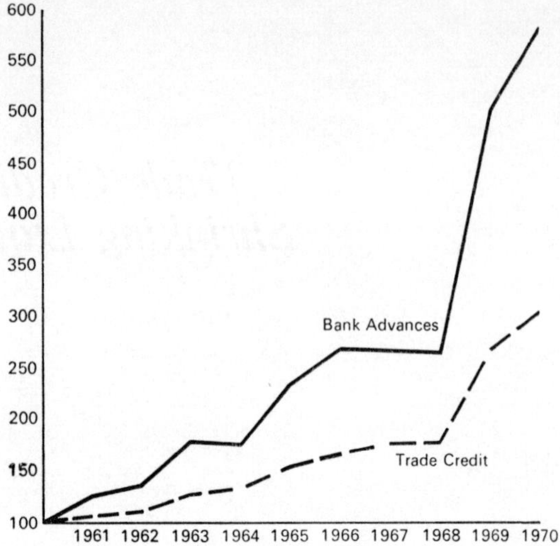

Figure 6. The growth of trade credit. Index (1960 = 100) shows comparative rise in trade credit and bank lending to manufacturing and distributive industry.

Based on figures produced by the Department of Trade and Industry. Data derived from regular sample of between 600 and 2,000 British companies.

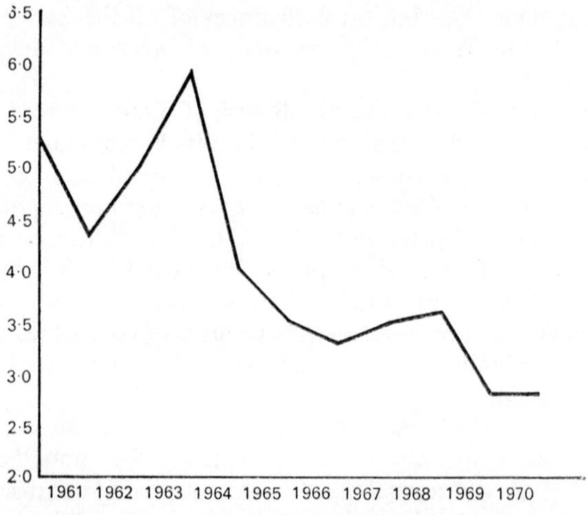

Figure. 7. The pattern of British Company Credit. Ratio of trade to bank credit. Source: Department of Trade and Industry. Data derived from regular sample of between 600 and 2,000 British companies.

Frequently, the companies taking the most credit in these conditions, may be the more shaky ones that the banks (also under pressure to reduce their lending) have turned away from their doors.

There is an unmistakable correlation between surges in the utilization of trade credit and increases in the number of company failures of all kinds. They are manifestations of the same economic condition—the 'credit squeeze'. As the accompanying graphs show (*see* Figures 6 and 7), the sharp rise in the outstanding level of both bank and trade

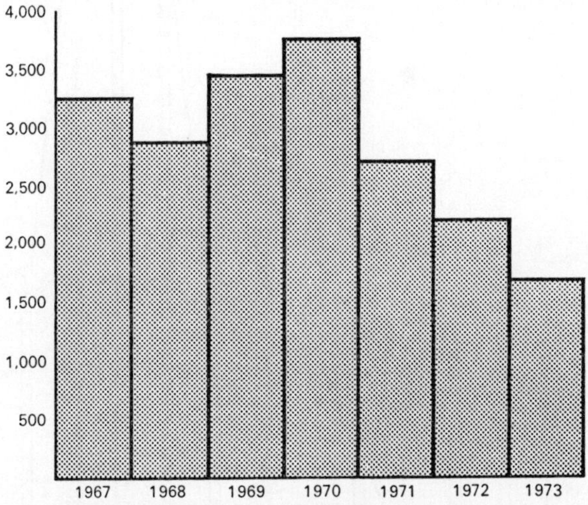

Figure 8. The insolvency rate. Bad debts and business failures notified to trade indemnity.

The first six months of 1973 shown as an annual rate.

credit during 1969 and 1970 was closely matched by the dramatic increase in the number of bad debtors, business failures and accounts for collection which were reported by Trade Indemnity (*see* Figures 8 and 9). Thus, while trade debt rose by about two-thirds (according to the best available figures) in the 1969–70 period, bad debtors and business failures jumped by some 29 per cent, and 'accounts notified for collection' soared nearly 75 per cent, by value, and 28 per cent by number (taking the average of the two years). The extent to which British corporate liquidity was under pressure in the later 1960s is also amply demonstrated. One prime indicator of corporate liquidity is the net acquisition or reduction of financial assets by industrial and commercial companies. Figures compiled by the Central Statistical

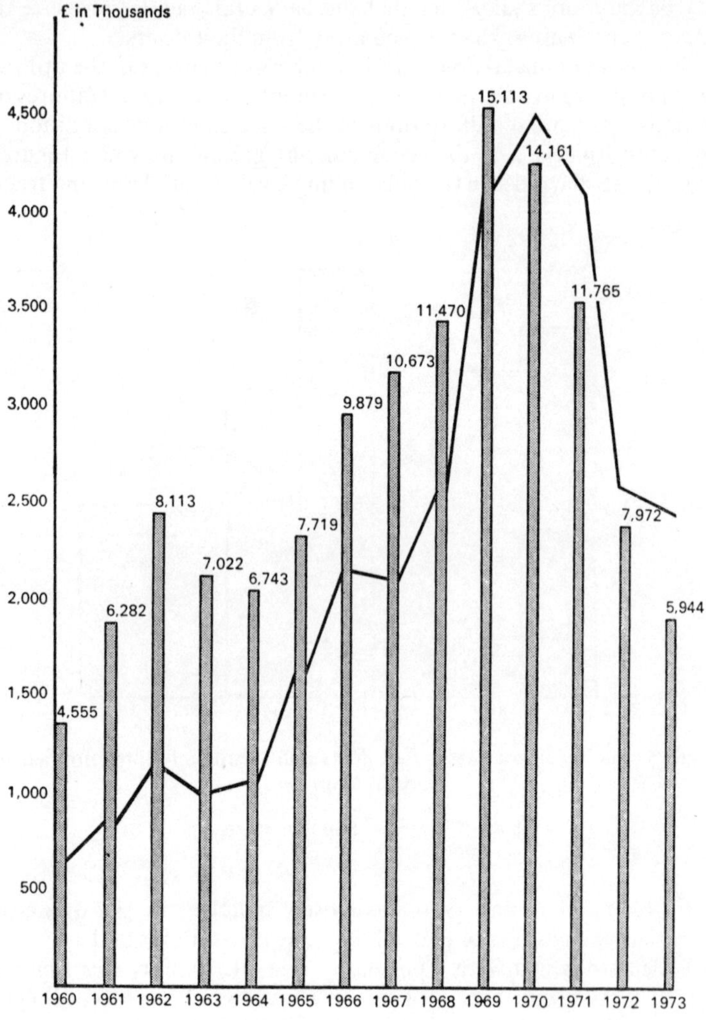

Figure 9. The unpaid debts.

Number and value of accounts notified to Trade Indemnity for collection. Trade Indemnity is the largest trade creditor insurer in Britain. Columns: number of accounts for collection; ——, value of account.

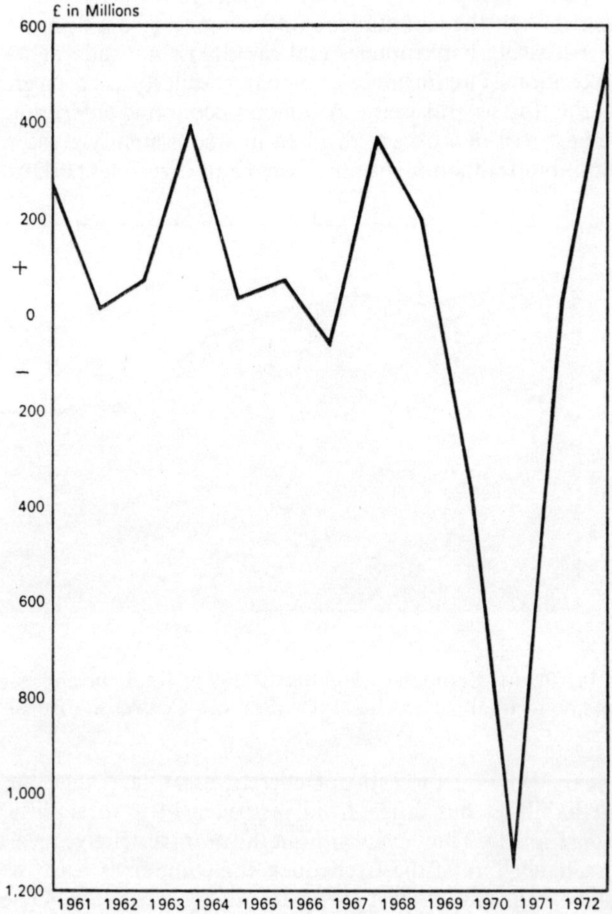

Figure 10. The financial position of British companies. Total net acquisition or reduction of financial assets of industrial and commercial corporate sector. Assets include notes and coin and treasury bills, tax reserve certificates, import deposits and deposits with banks and other financial institutions plus commercial bills. Source: Central Statistical Office.

Office (*see* Fig. 10) disclose an accelerating decline in the net financial assets of these companies in the three years following 1967.

Yet, although the simultaneous occurrence of declining financial assets, increasing bankruptcies and rapidly rising trade debts represents exceptional circumstances, company liquidity has been gradually contracting for several years. A difficult economic environment has for the best part of a decade resulted in a consistently greater rise in current liabilities than in current assets and investments. During the

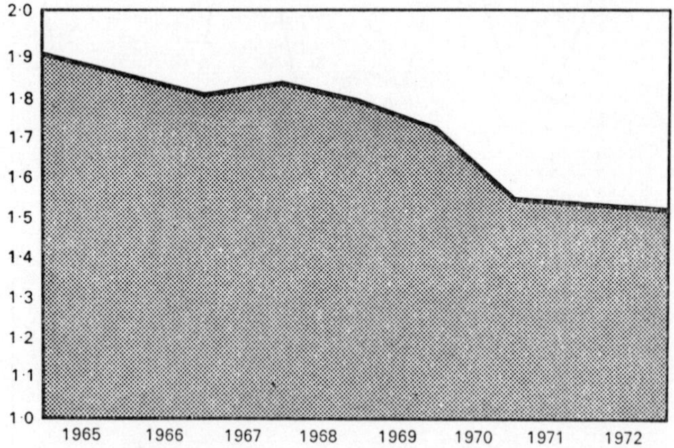

Figure 11. British Company Liquidity. Ratio of total current assets and investments to total current liabilities. Source: Central Statistical Office.

eight years 1964–72 the ratio of current assets and investments to current liabilities has fallen from just over 1·9:1 to slightly above 1·5:1 (*see* Fig. 11). Thus, even without the more restrictive measures of British Chancellors of the Exchequer, the company's ready cash has been shrinking. This at least partly accounts for the steady rise in the volume of trade credit, which occurs through economic 'stop' and 'go' policies.

The picture is not dissimilar in other industrial countries. In Europe, notably the Netherlands, West Germany, France, Sweden and Switzerland, the value of trade credit appears to range between three and four times that of bank lending to commercial and industrial customers. By contrast, in the U.S., the level of outstanding trade debts has remained consistently below that of commercial bank loans, although both forms of borrowing have risen very rapidly and almost in parallel (*see* Fig. 12). Over two decades the value of trade and bank credit in America expanded by something in the order of 400 per cent.

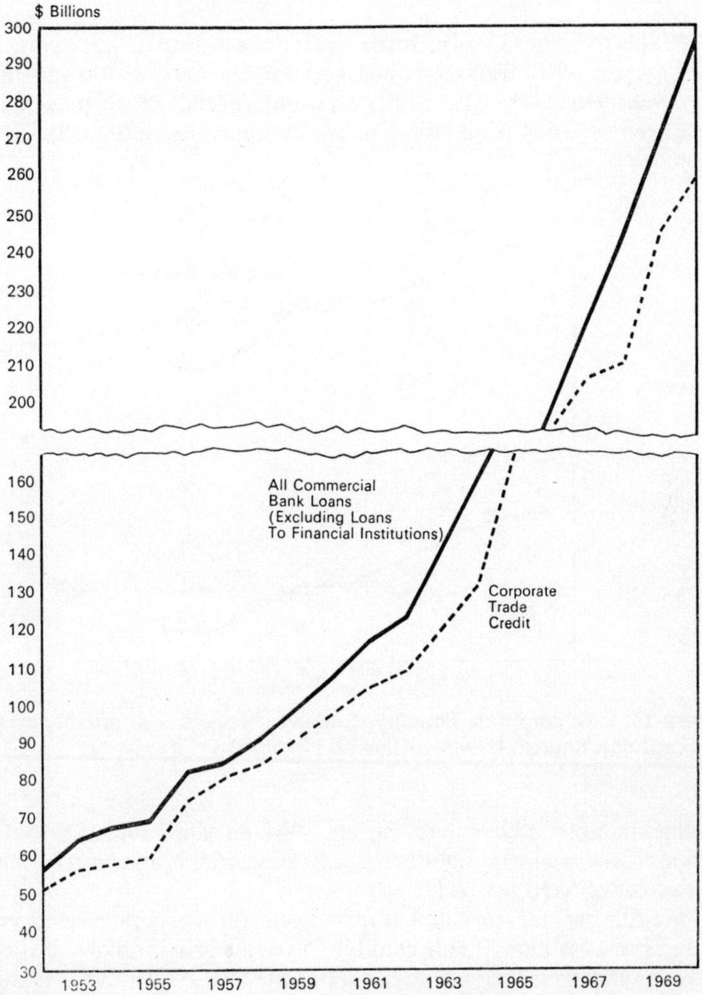

Figure 12. Expansion of U.S. bank loans and trade credit over two decades. Source: U.S. Securities and Exchange Commission and Federal Reserve.

The fact that bank lending has remained the larger is probably a reflection of differences in banking traditions between America and Europe.

The sharp rise in American trade credit owes little to inflation, which was comparatively well contained between the early 1950s and the later 1960s. However, like their British counterparts, U.S. corporations have been suffering from falling financial liquidity (*see* Fig. 13). This

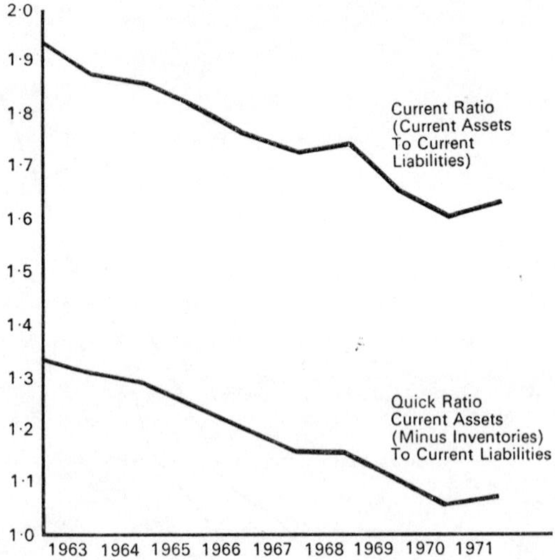

Figure 13. U.S. corporate liquidity. Liquidity ratios for all non-financial corporations. Source: U.S. Securities and Exchange Commission.

decline notably accelerated during 1964–66 and 1968–69—both periods associated with tight Federal Reserve credit policies resulting in a so-called 'credit crunch'.

This all has far reaching implications for corporate finances, budgets and cashflow. Trade credit involves the provision of goods or services on deferred payment terms. For the seller it means foregoing the use of money to which he is entitled, for the term that credit is outstanding. For the buyer, it represents the loan of resources, interest free.

The direct expense of granting credit is the cost of the finance needed, for the length of time it is outstanding. Unless the seller is in turn taking credit from his suppliers, he is either employing more money in the business than he otherwise would—perhaps even borrowing from his bank—or is necessarily obliged to temper his own expansion. Credit of £5,500 costs roughly £1·50 a day to finance at an annual interest rate of, say, 10 per cent. On thirty-day terms, the buyer is in effect receiving a gift of £45: on ninety-day terms, this rises to £135.

Against this, of course, the seller makes sales which, if the customer cannot pay cash, might otherwise not take place. As a result, he hopes to achieve a greater sales volume and a more economic use of production resources, leading to lower unit costs. But, equally, in industries which traditionally extend credit, the seller might lose sales if he did not provide the same terms as his competitors. The balance of advantage will depend on the particular circumstances of the business. For many small and medium-sized companies, already often undercapitalized, the cost of the extra sales attracted by generous discounts, can be higher than realized.

If, because of a shortage of working capital, they are forced to forfeit discounts offered for prompt payment by their own suppliers, this can be a heavy penalty. A discount of 2½ per cent foregone for the privilege of delaying payment for one month, is equal to borrowing at 30 per cent per annum. Conversely, offering discounts of this order to customers, in the hope of inducing speedy payment, is similarly expensive. When as a consequence, the cost of credit is built into the selling price, this intensifies inflationary pressures.

Over recent years, there has been a clear tendency for credit periods to lengthen. Within many industries, the traditional pattern of recognized credit periods has been breaking down. As a result, it must be assumed that liquidity problems have been generally more acute. A survey of 128 leading companies showed in 1971 that over a three year period the value of stocks and debtors rose by as much as 42 per cent, but the total amount of money which they employed increased only by 26 per cent. Although the survey was concerned with the larger company, the smaller firm would not seem to be any better placed. The survey showed an alarmingly slow turnover of money. The average turnover of funds was some 360 days, while for 15 of the very largest companies, the figure was 420 days. For many, overdrafts had become no longer temporary loans, but permanent working capital. Neither does passing on the problem to suppliers really solve the problem.

Successive credit squeezes and inflation would seem to be creating a new attitude towards trade debts, increasing the attraction of delaying payment. But the effects of this are unevenly distributed, favouring some to the disadvantage of others.

Further evidence of a general lengthening of trade credit terms is provided by investigations conducted in the engineering industry—the backbone of British industry and one of the single largest users of factoring. The investigation by the Engineering Industries Association of the situation in 1969, when the post-devaluation credit squeeze was nearing its worst, revealed that the level of trade debts outstanding at December 31, was some 92·5 per cent of turnover for the preceding three months. This was the highest percentage since these types of investigations were started, comparing with some 86·6 per cent of turn over for a similar period in 1968, and 78·0 per cent of turnover in a similar period of 1961.

In this case, although firms of all sizes were found to have suffered from the trend, the small concern was most severely affected, with its percentage of debts outstanding (on turnover for the last three months of 1969) increasing over the last quarter of 1968 by no less than 9·3 per cent. This compared with an overall increase for all firms, of 3·4 per cent. Interestingly, the investigation also found that while smaller firms had continued to discharge their debts at a constant rate, the larger companies had sharply extended the length of time that they took to pay their suppliers. The Engineering Industries Association told its members then that 'the general effect (of the lengthening credit terms) is severely to impede the provision of capital for expansion, to restrict the ability to finance future orders, to hamper our export trade and to promote a feeling of insecurity amongst management'. There has been no material sign since this investigation to suggest any reversal of the general trend.

That engineering companies are amongst the main clients of many factoring houses can be no coincidence. The normal cycle—stock, production, sales, cash receipts—can frequently take six months, especially where debtors take three months to pay. If this cyclical flow can be reduced from six months to, say, four months, it can effectively mean that each £1 of working capital can then finance £3 of sales per annum instead of £2 of sales—an increase of 50 per cent.

The 'feeling of insecurity amongst management', noted by the Engineering Industries Association, is no less than might be expected when future capital expenditure cannot be planned with any confidence because it is dependent on the vicissitudes of debt settlements; and when liquidity predictions cannot be made at any level of production because the availability of funds bears no relation to sales performance.

A further survey, this time conducted by the magazine *Business*, compared the length of trade credit offered by companies with the actual time taken by customers to pay their bills. This showed that whereas nearly 73 per cent of customers were normally requested to pay within one month, only 9 per cent did, on average, settle in 30 days or less, while 25 per cent of customers took over 61 days to pay their debts. This particular survey suggested that the smaller company was the worst culprit. Over 80 per cent of them were offered monthly settlement terms, but less than 10 per cent of these smaller companies made payments on time. The majority paid within 31 to 60 days, and a quarter of them held back settlement for two months. Either the payment terms offered by suppliers were irrelevant to the agreed practice and profit margins within their industries, or they were hopelessly inefficient at credit control and thus starved of vital cash. A recurring complaint was that large customers used the vast bureaucracy of their accounts departments deliberately to delay payment.

There was also a good deal of evidence in the survey to suggest that those companies which offered discounts as an inducement for prompt payment, found them more trouble than they were really worth. The time spent by accounts staff checking discount deductions and rejecting those which were either incorrectly calculated or deducted even after the qualifying time had elapsed, was often equally costly. Most companies appeared to offer discounts because it was traditional within the industry rather than because it was actually beneficial to do so. There was a general reluctance to charge interest on overdue accounts—as is the practice in the U.S.—because of the fear that this might generate ill will.

THE GAP—BETWEEN CREDIT GIVEN AND CREDIT TAKEN

The following is an analysis of trade credit, based on a survey of a wide cross-section of companies, which was conducted during a period of comparatively 'easy money' nationally. The results are expressed as a percentage and classified according to the size of customer.

	Small	*Medium*	*Large*	*Total*
Terms of Payment				
Week	—	1½	5	2½
2 weeks	—	—	1½	¾
Month	84	80	61	72¾
6 weeks*	10½	13	27½	18½
2 months	5½	5½	5	5½
Actual Credit Taken				
0–30 days	5¾	10	9½	9
31–60 days	65	58	66	62
61–90 days	23½	29	19½	25
Over 90 days	5¾	3	5	4

* This category includes those customers specifying 'end of month following month of delivery.' which is taken to be an average of six weeks credit.

Yet, this state of affairs is clearly unfair. A company suffering heavily from the effects of unpaid debts may be forced to put the overall cost of his goods up, penalizing both good and bad payers.

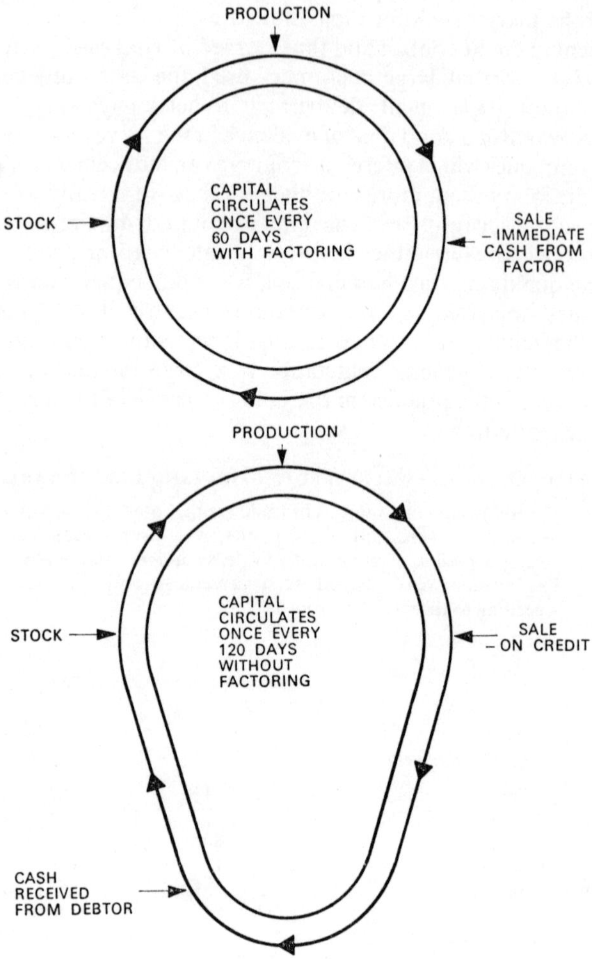

Figure 14. Turnover of working capital

Those buyers who do not take maximum credit will find themselves becoming part of the cost of providing finance to other buyers. As a consequence, the prompt payer is prevented from making optimum use of his own capital, and distortions are created. The cumulative effect must be to reduce the effective use of the nation's economic resources through the arbitrary, unplanned transfer of funds from one enterprise to another.

The provision of trade credit is essentially a marketing device which circumvents competition on price and quality of products and replaces it, in part, by financial inducements which can both protect the supplier and unfairly benefit some customers. It favours the company that has money rather than the company with the best products, and creates financial ties between suppliers and their customers. As a result, companies with little spare capital may not enjoy business which otherwise they might.

Trade Practice and Custom

In Britain, much of the trade credit granted is on monthly terms. Yet, it is obvious from the evidence, that this does not mean that payment will necessarily be forthcoming in 30 or 31 days from dispatch or receipt of goods. A common practice within British industry is for payment to be required on or before the last day of the month following the month in which goods are dispatched. For example, if goods are dispatched on November 5, the invoices would be payable by December 31. Thus, the buyer would receive 56 days credit. On average such terms provide 45 days credit. Again, the tradition may be for payments to be made at mid-month, say, on the 15th, with one full calendar month between dispatch and payment. Yet, although long established, many of these trade conventions are weakening. In the rag trade monthly account terms were usual, but now it is becoming widely accepted that two months grace is taken before payment is made. It can be even longer if the transaction is financed by a trade bill. It is not unknown for an order to be taken initially on open-credit terms, and then to be subsequently financed by a trade bill, providing as much as five months credit in total.

This type of situation can arise particularly in the fur trade and in connection with the seasonal side of the rag trade where payment for goods is often delayed until the autumn when they are resold. One area in which rather strict credit terms were observed was in the sale of raw materials for textile manufacture (wool tops and pre-spun cotton). If an invoice was paid within seven days the standard discount was 3¾ per cent, the discount then being reduced in stages according to how long the buyer took to pay—2½ per cent if paid at the end of the month, 1¼ per cent after two months, disappearing completely after three months. However, payment terms in this sector are slacker now.

The few trades where strict payment disciplines are still maintained tend to be those dealing in raw materials of a perishable nature—meat, fish and fruit and vegetables. It is usual in these trades to pay for goods within a matter of days. The hosiery trade, too, is an example of a sector with clearly defined payment practices. A 3 per cent discount is offered where payment is made within seven days of dispatch and $2\frac{1}{2}$ per cent obtainable if payment is made promptly after receipt of the invoice.

In contrast to the examples of lengthening payment periods in some industries, the steel industry presents an illustration of where the

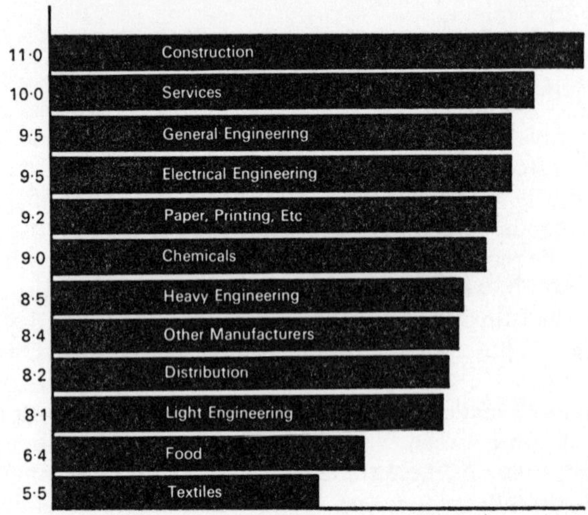

Figure 15. The time they take to pay. Average credit taken in individual industries (in weeks). Based on an independent survey

process has been reversed. In 1971, the British Steel Corporation made a policy decision to keep credit periods to stockholders on a tight rein. However, this simply increased the difficulties of the stockholders who were unable to apply the same kind of pressure on their own customers. Perhaps it is no coincidence that, along with textile and engineering firms, one of the other principal sectors using factoring is steel stockholding.

There are some sectors, like the chemical industry where, although discounts are not widely used, the tradition is still mostly observed for settlement to be made at the end of the month following the month in which the invoice is received.

Again, in some parts of the dress trade, all dispatches up to the 19th of any month are settled on the 10th of the next month. Thus, in this trade the average terms are about 36 days—i.e. if the mid-point of an account running from 20 October to 19 November is 4 November then an average 36 days credit will be extended before payment is due on 10 December. So, in this trade, average credit terms are 20 per cent less than in many other trades. Where carpets are concerned, all invoices issued within a given month are due on the 20th of the following month. This means an average 35 to 36 days credit are provided, in effect the same as for the dress trade, only calculated from a different point.

If every customer paid on time, the debts owed in the carpet trade would turn over ten times each year, whereas, on the more common credit terms used elsewhere, debts are turned over only eight times a year. From this it follows that, in order to finance the same volume of turnover, 25 per cent more capital is needed than in the carpet trade.

Discounts are frequently offered in many trades, particularly by medium-sized companies. They vary widely in amount and $2\frac{1}{2}$ or $3\frac{3}{4}$ per cent are quite common. However, some suppliers are willing to offer 5 or even 6 per cent to customers who settle within seven days, while even 10 per cent discounts might be forthcoming for cash settlement. These discounts will be reduced in stages as credit terms lengthen, until they are eliminated altogether. The available evidence suggests that between a third and a half of all companies in the manufacturing and service industries (excluding retail trades) offer some kind of discount. But, perhaps, only half of all transactions are settled sufficiently quickly to qualify for discounts. The conclusion must be that a large proportion of customers find it more advantageous to stall their payments than to avail themselves of the reduced price offered for early payment.

This weakening of traditional payment disciplines, together with an apparently universal reduction in corporate liquidity and the advantages, in an inflationary era, of owing money, have contributed to the growth of factoring. It represents one method of bringing sales accounts back under control. An intimate knowledge of trade customs and practices is elementary to factoring. Frequently, the factor has different members of his staff specializing in one or two trades or industries. They will be aware that the average debt payment time in the printing industry is around 63 days and in engineering 59 days. They will additionally know which firms consistently take longer than the average to settle and which make irregular payments unrelated to any specific purchase.

The employment of techniques like the open-item system of sales ledger accounting, which gives a breakdown of each account by invoice and age of individual debt, allows the dilatory payers to be identified. This, together with tighter credit limits and more efficient collection methods, can help arrest and reverse a deterioration in a company's debt turn, against the national and international trend. At a stroke, the liquidity position might be substantially improved, the cashflow boosted, budgeting enhanced and capital utilization promoted.

The need to take a firm grip on trade credit, and achieve a more economical use of resources becomes more urgent with Britain's greater commercial integration with the European Community and unimpaired admission to huge new markets on which its businessmen will come to depend. Like the traditional home market, business transactions will be largely conducted on an open-account basis. With money owed by customers based, perhaps, in Hamburg, Turin, or Lyons, the British supplier will find the cost of continuous assessment and collection of accounts rise sharply. But anything less than a firm rigorous approach to debtors could lead to a marked lengthening in the debt turn and an uncomfortable reduction in liquidity. Trade credit, in fact, could prove the fatal flaw in the strategies of numerous British companies intent on grasping new opportunities and penetrating European markets.

6 A Profile of the Factors

Factoring in its present form came to Britain towards the close of 1960. In November of that year, Mr Charles Harding, president of Meinhard & Co, one of the larger New York factoring houses, flew into London to help establish a subsidiary operation in conjunction with a City group called Alexandria Finance Company. Although their offspring proved to be only short-lived, it marked the beginning of an era. The formation of other factoring companies quickly followed.

The impetus behind the Meinhard–Alexandria operation came from a desire primarily to facilitate Anglo-North American trade. International trade was generally enjoying a strong growth and many American businessmen found themselves selling to Europe for the first time. But they were unused to the documentation and methods of payment involved and wanted to be paid on an open-account basis like that to which they were accustomed for inter-state commerce. The transplanting of factoring to America's main overseas trading partners presented itself as the most promising answer to the problem.

Not surprisingly, it was a technique which attracted a number of British confirming houses who, because of a shift in the country's trading patterns away from the colonies, were seeking financial diversification. It also aroused the interest of several people in the field of credit insurance who viewed it as a natural extension of their activities and who were able to provide valuable experience in assessing the creditworthiness of companies. In this fertile environment factoring rapidly took root.

Despite its inauspicious early history, factoring later began to appeal to the major clearing banks as a means of broadening the range of financial facilities that they offered their customers. Led by National Provincial in 1968, the big banks started to become participants in the industry. Within two years this trend was followed by the London-based subsidiaries of the large U.S. banks. Many of these London subsidiaries were established to exploit the blossoming Eurodollar market which was centred on the City. But as the Eurodollar market alone was not enough to sustain all of these subsidiaries, some of the more adventurous began developing sterling operations and expanded into domestic British financing—leasing, factoring and merchant banking.

There follows a brief profile of each of the major factoring houses. It is not an exhaustive list of factors; there are several small and essentially provincial factors scattered across the country. Those that feature below are the larger, national houses, chiefly based in London or the South East of England and backed, in most cases, by prestigious financial institutions. By 1972, there were eleven principal factoring houses (there have in fact been twelve, but not all conducting business simultaneously). However, mergers within the industry have reduced their number to nine.

International Factors

Mr Harding's sojourn in November 1960 was followed less than two months later by the formation of another, unconnected factoring enterprise. One of the moving spirits behind this was the First National Bank of Boston, which had been one of the pioneers of modern factoring in the U.S. This bank wished to extend its activities overseas. It joined with M. Samuel and Co., a London merchant bank, and Tozer Kemsley & Millbourn, a confirming house (which had been conducting business not so greatly dissimilar to factoring in the Commonwealth for some years) to set up International Factors Ltd.

Tozer Kemsley had in fact started a factoring operation called Towergate Securities a few months earlier and this became the vehicle for the formation of International Factors Ltd. The latter company started life with an authorized capital of £300,000 and an issued capital of £200,000, half provided by Tozer Kemsley and a quarter each by the other two partners. It was the first factoring company to be successfully launched and was still by far the largest more than a dozen years later.

However, in common with most of its contemporaries, its history was chequered. In August 1968 when the Lloyds and Scottish Finance group (owned by Lloyds Bank and the Royal Bank of Scotland) bought a 70 per cent interest in International Factors, it had notched up an accumulated deficit of some £450,000 on a capital of not much more. M. Samuel had, in the meantime, merged with another merchant bank, Phillip Hill Higginson, to become Hill Samuel and readily agreed to

THE MAJOR FACTORS IN BRITAIN

Company	*Year founded*	*Shareholders*	*Size of holding %*
Arbuthnot Factors	1964	Arbuthnot Latham & Co. (I.C.F.C. has 21%, Philadelphia National Bank 8%, and Chartered Bank 8% in Arbuthnot Latham & Co.)	100
Barclay's factoring division	1972	Barclays Bank, through Barclays Export and Finance Company	100
BankAmerica-WilliamsGlyn Factors	1970	Bank of America	51
		Williams and Glyn's Bank	39
		Mr J. Kenneth Holland	10
Credit Factoring International (formed to replace the business of Portland Group Factors, originally founded in 1963)	1970	National Westminster Bank, through Credit Factoring International	100
H. & H. Factors (bought Allied Factors in 1972)	1964	Walter E. Heller International Corporation	63
		Continental Illinois National Bank	10
		Hambros Bank	25
		Others	2
International Factors (started life as Towergate Securities)	1960	Lloyds and Scottish Finance	75
		First National Bank of Boston	25
Alex Lawrie Factors (took over Bankers Trust Factors in 1973)	1963	Alex Lawrie Holdings (which is in turn 72% owned by Walter Duncan & Goodricke Ltd, 20% by Banque Belge, and 8% by Mr N. Grant)	100
Mercantile Credit factoring sub-division	1965	Mercantile Credit	100
Griffin Factors (absorbed business of Midland-Citibank Factors in 1973)	1963	Midland Bank	100
Other companies involved in debtor finance			
Goode Durrant & Murray	late 1950s	Goode Durrant & Murray (Consolidated) (in turn controlled by Goode Durrant & Murray Group Ltd.)	100
London Bridge Finance	1959	Hill Samuel	100

sell its share interest. Tozer Kemsley's shareholding fell to 5 per cent; the First National Bank of Boston became the largest minority shareholder, possessing the remainder of the equity.

By its twelth birthday, International Factors employed some 140 people to service 60 clients with 13,000 to 15,000 current customers, or 'live debtors'. Its files covered between 60,000 and 80,000 firms. Nearly a fifth of its clients were publicly quoted companies. Total turnover was, in 1973, some £70M, and profits climbed in that year from £424,000 to £452,000. Because of a setback in overseas markets for the knitwear division of a large textile group, the export turnover of International Factors had slipped to £12M in 1972, having grown very rapidly during the previous four years to reach £15M. Import turnover was running at about £4M per annum. Moreover, the First National Bank of Boston has pursued its expansionist programme and International Factors Ltd is now a member of a world-wide network, the International Factors Group.

Of the British company's turnover, all but about £8M was derived from main-line factoring: the balance resulted from invoice discounting. This side of the business had been contributed by its Lloyds and Scottish parent which had amongst its interests a company that had formerly traded as Olds Discount. This in turn owned an invoice discounting subsidiary called Trade Sales. The activities of the latter were transferred to International Factors and are now conducted by its subsidary Confidential Invoice Discounting Ltd.

The possession by Lloyds and Scottish of three-quarters of International Factors in Britain (Tozer Kemsley sold its remaining 5 per cent interest to Lloyds and Scottish) had a significant influence on the factoring company's affairs. Banking disciplines and more stringent credit criteria were adopted. In addition, International Factors was able to tap the huge resources and branch networks of the two parent banks. Greater management expertise was also injected. Yet its operating finance is derived independently, by borrowing on the City's wholesale money markets as this exerts an increased discipline on its affairs. An essentially service-orientated factor, it places somewhat less emphasis on advancing funds. It uses the Finance Houses Association base rate as the starting point for calculating its interest charges on advances. In spite of the advantages of the parent bank's branch networks, International Factors has pursued expansion through a strong regional policy and several of its own branches have been opened throughout the country.

Griffin Factors

The years 1963 to 1966 saw the establishment of several factoring houses. Shield Factors (later called Griffin Factors following its merger with a competitor), set up in September 1963, is one of the oldest after International Factors. Like International, one of Shield's founding shareholders was an old established confirming house, Anglo-African Shipping Co., (S.A.). The initial involvement of a merchant bank, in this case N. M. Rothschild & Sons, was a second similarity between these two forerunners in the factoring industry. Anglo-African and Rothschild owned 35 and 20 per cent respectively of Shield Factors. Several other financial institutions were also successfully tempted to participate in these early stages. Shield was provided with a prestigious list of shareholders, including Eagle Star Insurance (15 per cent interest), I.C.F.C. Ltd (15 per cent), merchant bankers Kleinwort Benson (7½ per cent) and insurance brokers C. T. Bowring & Co. (7½ per cent).

By 1972, Shield had an estimated turnover of £30M–35M—about 10 per cent derived from export business—and a staff of about 100, some shared with Anglo-African. Its operations included 'with recourse' and 'without recourse' factoring in addition to 'notification' and 'non-notification' activities. Moreover, it was one of the founder members of Factors Chain International, a world-wide network of 'independent' factors not connected with one of the three multinational groupings.

It was as late as March 1973 that Shield forged a partnership with the Midland Bank. Three years earlier Midland and the First National City Bank of New York had formed Midland-Citibank Factors, with an initial capital of £2M. But this arrangement, which proved less than fully satisfactory, was terminated amicably before the Midland-Citibank factoring turnover had scarcely reached £5M (including some invoice discounting business). In a bid to capture a larger proportion of the factoring industry, Midland arranged to merge its factoring interests with those of Shield. It bought out the First National City bank of New York and acquired a 50 per cent interest in Shield—a deal said to have cost some £500,000. Anglo-African Shipping increased its own stake in Shield to 50 per cent, parting company with the other, former owners. The name 'Griffin Factors' was chosen for the new, merged group as a griffin had long been the Midland Bank's own symbol. In October 1974 Midland bought out Anglo-African's shareholding and Griffin became their wholly-owned subsidiary.

Credit Factoring

At about the same time that Shield came into existence, Portland Group Factors was being formed by two brothers called Citroen, partly drawing on the experience of one of them in the accountancy profession. Although it grew rapidly, its systems proved less than completely adequate to cope with the expansion, and the difficulties this engendered exemplified many of the industry's early weaknesses. Management controls were too lax, and it acquired an ill-assorted group of clients. Also, advances were often unjustifiably large.

A couple of years after Portland's formation, National Provincial Bank acquired, through its subsidiary North Central Finance, a 20 per cent interest in the company—the first clearing bank to show a positive interest in factoring, albeit an indirect one. By this time Portland's turnover was nearing £25M. Within a short space of time, National Provincial's interest was stepped up to a controlling 75 per cent. But radical changes were on the way in other areas of banking; National Provincial merged with the Westminster Bank. This was to have far-reaching repercussions both on Portland and the factoring industry. The newly formed National Westminster Bank took an increasingly close day-to-day interest in Portland's affairs and was critical of what it found. It purchased the balance of the equity that it did not own and established a completely new operation to replace the existing business, investing heavily in the project.

The surgery was brutal. Portland's 80 clients were pruned back to less than 10, leaving just a rump on which to rebuild. The name given to the new Company was Credit Factoring. Turnover, which in May 1968 had been £25M was transferred to the new company at a level reduced to £4M. Not until the end of 1972 was turnover again running at the £30M level; twelve months later this had been doubled. It was decided not to change the systems immediately. Instead, National Westminster spent over two years establishing a fully comprehensive computer system tailored to suit an elaborate factoring programme. Around £1M to £2M was invested in the project, to provide capacity for an aggregate turnover running into hundreds of millions of pounds —comparable to the turnover of the major New York factors.

Credit Factoring is amongst those in the industry that places greatest stress on the sales ledger, credit insurance and other services, rather than on advancing funds. Nearly half of its 40 clients were not, for example, drawing any advance funds at the end of 1972. Another third required only part of the funds available to them ahead of the average maturity date. Consequently, Credit Factoring was advancing money against only about 20 per cent of the overall debts it factored. Because of its tendency to attract the larger client, the average turnover handled was higher than is usual, at £750,000. Several of its clients were public companies and a few were numbered amongst Britain's 100 largest companies—two were amongst the top 20. It operates almost exclusively on a 'notification' and 'without recourse' basis.

But in one specific direction Credit Factoring is unique. It is the only

British factor which has attempted to establish its own international network, through Credit Factoring International, which started as a subsidiary. It has so far opened offices in some 14 countries, serving 17 separate markets (some offices serve two countries). Although, in the early years, the intention was that these offices should service British exports to those countries, the system was designed ultimately to accommodate a multi-directional flow of business. Unlike the other multinational factoring groups, Credit Factoring did not initially seek partners in other countries, preferring to train its own personnel and administer all the foreign branches within one standard discipline, using a central international clearing system in Britain. Only when the matrix was firmly established did Credit Factoring countenance foreign links with banks prepared to work within the developed framework. In 1972, the first of such links was announced.

This was with Credito Italiano, a leading Italian bank. The linkup was accomplished through the sale to Credito Italiano of a 50 per cent share in the Milan operation. This opened the way for the new partners to factor Italian exports. However, Credit Factoring continued to run the operation from its Feltham office. Subsequently, further such deals were negotiated, two of them in Asia—in Hong Kong and Singapore. In the former, its partner was The Chartered Bank which acquired 49 per cent of the new enterprise in the colony. Essentially, it was formed to service Hong Kong exports to America and Europe. In Singapore, Credit Factoring was joined in the establishment of a new enterprise by The Chartered Bank (with 35 per cent of the local company) and, more enigmatically, the Pacific International Lines Steamship Company (with 15 per cent).

But, the most significant development in this programme was the establishment of C. F. International Inc. in the U.S. This was jointly set up by Credit Factoring and a large American factor, John P. Maguire, owned by Provident National Bank of Philadelphia and which had in 1972 a turnover of $665M. C. F. International Inc. is physically located adjacent to the offices of John P. Maguire, handling the America factor's exports but with the new company's business conducted as part of Credit Factoring's unified system. This arrangement thus linked a major factor on each side of the Atlantic in a potentially powerful relationship. Of the British turnover handled by Credit Factoring, nearly a quarter was, by 1972, bound for overseas markets and the proportion predicted to reach a half within two years. The increasing significance of the international side of the total business, was reflected in a restructuring of Credit Factoring at the beginning of 1974. Under the new structure Credit Factoring International—hitherto a subsidiary of Credit Factoring Ltd, responsible for the non-British business— became the parent umbrella company of the organization controlling the various world-wide operations including those of Credit Factoring Ltd in Britain.

Alex Lawrie Factors

Following the formation of Portland Group Factors, three other factoring houses opened their doors for business in rapid succession, bringing the total at that time to six. The three newcomers were Alex Lawrie Factors, Arbuthnot Lock Factors, and H. & H. Factors. Alex Lawrie was in fact incorporated in 1962, but its trading life effectively began towards the close of the following year. It was launched with a capital of £10,000, half each subscribed by Alex Lawrie & Co., and International Factors Corporation of Montreal (not to be confused with the British and world-wide International Factors group of companies associated with the First National Bank of Boston; the name is only coincidentally the same and there is no connection).

Alex Lawrie Factors is in the middle rank of the industry with a turnover in 1973 of some £50M. The foundation of the original parent company, Alex Lawrie & Co., was steeped in Britain's colonial past. It was started in 1878 as an East India merchant, with particular interest in tea, having plantations in India, and became a public company in 1935. Like the confirming houses which were at the forefront of factoring initially, Alex Lawrie was keenly looking for an avenue of financial diversification, when it was approached in 1962 by a leading personality from International Factors Corporation of Montreal, a shareholder in one of Lawrie's tea companies, with a proposition to set up a jointly owned factoring company in Britain. This proposal was brought to fruition, but difficult exchange control regulations later led to the Montreal factor withdrawing from the enterprise.

However, about this time—the middle 1960s—another Indian tea company, Walter Duncan & Goodricke, was also seeking diversification, and succeeded in taking over Lawrie. As a consequence, Alex Lawrie & Co. was to become the financial holding company for the Walter Duncan financial interests, which have been expanded to include leasing, property and merchant banking, in addition to factoring. The Lawrie tea estates were transferred to Walter Duncan, whose other interests now include transport and warehousing. This re-shuffle has made it possible for the Lawrie holding company to be re-floated on the London Stock Exchange, once more a quoted company.

In many ways, Alex Lawrie Factors is regarded by the rest of the industry as an 'outsider'. It has developed along rather different lines to its counterparts and its methods tend to vary from theirs. For much of its history, it was the only factor without any merchant bank or clearing bank link. Consequently, it had to obtain finance through standard overdraft and credit line arrangements with City institutions. Its systems owe much to the model of its Montreal co-founder, suitably modified to British conditions.

One major difference between its operation and that of other factors has been its tendency to obtain extra security for advances through adoption of a charge on the assets of its clients. Unlike some other factors, it is essentially finance-orientated in its services. Moreover, most of its business is on a 'with recourse' basis—a feature it shares with only one other member of the industry. But it also conducts 'non-notification' and invoice discounting operations. Although under the non-notification system the client's own name still appears on its invoices, the customer is informed that the sales ledger is kept at Banbury, which is in fact where Alex Lawrie's main office is housed. This is kept secret by the use of separate telephone lines at Banbury (and differently coloured telephones to avoid mistake) where customer enquiries are dealt with by Lawrie staff acting in the name of the client.

The 'with recourse' principle can often permit Lawrie to accommodate clients with sales considerably below what is normally acceptable in factoring, perhaps £50,000, rather than £100,000; and selling to smaller-sized customers for whom it is impossible to arrive at any meaningful credit rating. The factoring commission is related to the amount of paper work that a client requires, and is calculated on a sliding scale—another difference from the methods of other factors. Lawrie's overseas turnover is comparatively small, amounting to only about 5 or 10 per cent of its turnover. In the absence of the kind of branch networks that the big banks have brought to factoring, it has opened a number of regional offices. Even so, with nearly 200 clients in 1973, it handled one of the largest portfolios in the industry.

A merchant bank has been formed by the group to enable it to provide a greater range of services to its clients. These facilities were extended with the purchase of a sales ledger bureau-cum-computer advisory specialist, a move which takes Lawrie closer to its concept of a 'financial supermarket'.

It was in the summer of 1973 that Lawrie took over Bankers Trust Factors, owned principally by the Bankers Trust, an American bank, and General Accident Fire and Life Corporation. This particular factoring house had been set up two years earlier when U.S. banks had been enthusiastically entering the British factoring industry. Twenty-four months before that, Bankers Trust had also joined the stampede to buy American independent factoring houses, purchasing Coleman Factors in the U.S.

Although Bankers Trust Factors had a generous initial capital, its performance proved disappointing for its shareholders. The management displayed insufficient determination in controlling overheads and the various parties in the enterprise did not achieve the partnership necessary to ensure the efficient running of the operation. Bankers Trust and General Accident (the first composite insurance company to take a positive interest in factoring) cut their losses and withdrew their investments. But, being an operation conducted on 'with recourse' lines, their factoring business held attractions for Alex Lawrie, which bought the company, its £9M turnover, 12 factoring clients and 7 invoice discounting clients. Re-named Independent Factors Ltd, this acquisition will continue to be run for some years as a separate entity for tax purposes. This takeover was followed by a, perhaps, even more important event for Alex Lawrie Factors. This was when Banque Belge Ltd, the British subsidiary of Société Générale de Banque S.A., one of the major continental banks, bought a 20 per cent interest in the Alex Lawrie group. Still without any established banking connections, this move opened the way for Lawrie to obtain some of its financial requirements. A million pounds was immediately put at the Lawrie group's disposal by Banque Belge. With this deal, the factoring industry lost the last of the 'independents', unconnected with an established bank or finance house.

Arbuthnot Factors

True to the general pattern, one of the co-founders of Arbuthnot Factors was a confirming house, S. H. Lock. The other was a City merchant bank, Arbuthnot Latham. Originally, called Arbuthnot Lock Factors, the name has twice been changed, having for a time been known as A. L. Factors. Behind the confirming house involvement lay the same assumptions that drew others of its kind into factoring notably that their experience in related fields could be of value to the new institutions that they were establishing. But as some others found, in reality a completely different set of disciplines had to be devised for factoring. Arbuthnot Factors became wholly owned by Arbuthnot Latham when Lock's parent company was taken over.

Although it entered the field comparatively early, it has not experienced the growth of some of its contemporaries, and its turnover was running at only about £10M at the beginning of 1973. Of this only a small proportion resulted from overseas business since it has mainly concentrated on the domestic market. Like some of the other factors, its operations were less than a complete success at first. The mechanics of its operations were somewhat unwieldy, conducted both in London and Hastings. This required twice-daily delivery of invoices by rail and courier from the coast to the City. When the information had been computerized the results were either relayed by telex or physically transported back to Hastings. This could cause delays of up to 48 hours. However, this regime has since been changed.

Initially, its service was based on 'non-notification, with recourse' factoring. But later on Arbuthnot adopted the disclosed, 'without recourse' system. It also conducts invoice discounting business. Being one of the smaller factors (it employs a comparatively small staff of 20 to 30) it both insures against fraud and reinsures the trade debts that it factors. Its 50 clients and 10 year-history is evidence that there remains an essential role for the smaller factoring house that can accommodate clients that are chary of being factored by the group with whom they bank.

H. & H. Factors

H. & H. Factors began trading in 1964. In its case, it was the confirming house Keep Bros. Ltd, of Birmingham that played a paramount part in the formation. A little before this event, Credit Consultants, a specialist firm of credit insurance brokers and consultants, was considering new forays in this area, having gained much experence from its part in setting up the London Bridge Finance operation. Together, Credit Consultants, Keep Bros., and a number of individuals in the credit insurance field, established in 1962 the company Keep Bros. (Trading Capital), run on similar lines to London Bridge. However, it lacked sufficient finance and, in any case, the more simple, factoring-type of operation was moving to the centre of the stage.

To obtain more finance, a successful approach was made to the City merchant bank of Hambros, which took an equity interest in Keep Bros. (Trading Capital). But events quickly overtook this move. Inspired by the logic of combining credit insurance with finance in a factoring package, several of the individual backers behind Keep Bros, (Trading Capital), attempted to drum up support for the idea from a syndicate of merchant banks. This attempt failed. But simultaneously, the Walter E. Heller company, one of the largest factors in New York, was investigating the possibilities of expanding outside of the U.S. The result was the formation of H. & H. Factors. Heller became the major shareholder and Hambros took a 25 per cent stake. Credit Consultants Ltd, and Continental Illinois National Bank and Trust Company of Chicago, one of the largest American banks, each had minority interests in the new factor.

Within eight years, the factored turnover of H. & H. was close to £30M. In 1972 it made factoring history by becoming the first to be involved in a factoring industry merger, absorbing Allied Factors. The latter was itself formed in 1966. It was owned by Allied Finance &

Insurance Services, a public company, and backed by Sir Isaac Wolfson's General Guarantee Corporation, from whom it obtained its main line of finance—around £1·5M. At its peak, Allied Factors had a turnover of £14M and employed a staff of 60, conducting 'without recourse' business.

However, Allied was finding it more difficult than some of its competitors to resolve many of the problems that factoring had thrown up. An attempt at reorganization proved less than completely successful because, without direct bank support, it lacked the necessary cash. Unselective in its clients and still suffering from two cases of fraud and the high costs of a new computer system, Allied was losing money when it merged with H. & H. Factors.

The deal was effected through the purchase by H. & H. Factors of Allied's £2M book debts and the additional payment to the former owners of £112,000 for goodwill. At that time H. & H. was of a similar size to Allied and was also making losses because of a major client failure. The transference of clients from one factor to the other immediately posed delicate problems. Such an event could be expected to create a considerable sense of insecurity for the clients. This merger is still the largest to have occurred in the industry.

Some pruning of Allied's portfolio of clients was inevitable, but proved less severe than that which followed National Westminster's revamping of Portland Group Factors. But it prompted a review of H. & H. Factor's own client list. The result, a year after the merger, was a portfolio of 100 clients with between 10,000 and 20,000 customers; an average client turnover of £300,000; and a staff of 80.

Being part of a world-wide network, export-import business is given a high priority by H. & H. Factors, which has energetically attempted to exploit Britain's accession to the European Community and to increase its penetration of overseas markets. Around a quarter of its turnover is accounted for by such business—of this, 25 per cent represents imports, a fast growing element in its foreign trade activities. H. & H. Factors concentrates on 'notification, without recourse' factoring and has opened regional offices.

But in one respect the Walter E. Heller operation in Britian was unique in factoring. As an additional service it established a central Marketing Bureau in London to promote and assist trade between its clients, factored throughout the world by the many subsidiaries and associate companies in the Heller network (of which H. & H. is one). The intention was to introduce importers and exporters of various products, matching their prices, delivery and short-term credit needs, and to help to generate business for Heller's tens-of-thousands of customers. Having stimulated business and matched the requirements of the parties, the local factoring companies in the countries concerned made collections and payments in the normal way—a concept which added a new dimension to factoring. This operation, however, has now been transferred to the U.S. where Heller already conducts a similar marketing business.

Mercantile Credit

Mercantile Credit (Factors) was one of the last of those to be set up during the first wave of factoring company formations which took place in the early and middle 1960s. Initially it was formed as a wholly owned subsidiary of Mercantile Credit, the finance house and not surprisingly therefore, was essentially finance orientated, viewing factoring as just an extension of the group's money lending operations. When in 1973 Mercantile Credit became a statutory bank, it bought the assets of its factoring arm and absorbed the business into its industrial and financial division, which also conducts hire purchase, leasing and secured lending operations. Apart from Alex Lawrie, it is the only factoring operation which currently specialises in 'with recourse' business. It also provides an invoice discounting service. The wholesale reappraisal of clients which has preoccupied much of the industry in recent years, has not been avoided by Mercantile. During 1972, factoring turnover was reduced by a quarter, to some £12M. The involvement of Mercantile Credit factoring in overseas trade is also very modest. It undertakes such business to accommodate clients, but does not seek it out. Membership of Factors Chain International became difficult for Mercantile because its procedures were incompatible with most of its counterparts, and it withdrew.

BankAmerica-WilliamsGlyn Factors

The second wave of factoring company formations began in 1970, although the Lloyds and National Westminster involvement in the industry formed a bridge between this later stage and the earlier period which ended with the establishment of Mercantile Credit (Factors) in 1965. Three factors were formed in 1970, each with American bank support. However, as recorded above, two of these new factors—Midland-Citibank Factors and Bankers Trust Factors—have subsequently been merged with older houses.

The third of the 1970 trio was Bank America Finance (Factors), set up by the Bank of America, the world's largest bank. It was joined in the new enterprise a year later by Williams and Glyn's Bank, one of the smaller British clearing banks, which paid £191,000 for its 39 per cent share in the factor. Bank of America maintained a 51 per cent controlling interest and the balance was held by the factor's managing director. The factoring house was then renamed BankAmerica-WilliamsGlyn Factors. Providing 'notification' and 'without recourse' services, plus invoice discounting facilities, the new company began to expand rapidly, and by early 1973 its turnover was running at an annual rate of some £18M. Apart from its British factoring venture, the Bank of America's other interests in this field do not extend beyond a receivables financing operation in California and a small-scale 'old-line' operation. In spite of this limited experience, success for its factoring enterprise in Britain could lead to similar subsidiaries being formed elsewhere in Europe.

Barclays

Finally, there occurred in March 1972, the development which had been long expected and widely speculated upon, the entry into factoring of Barclays Bank, which thus completed the involvement of all the major London clearing banks. However, Barclays neither created a new self-contained factoring subsidiary nor purchased an interest in an existing factoring house. Instead, a factoring division was created within what was subsequently called Barclays Export and Finance Company (B.E.A.F.C.O.), a wholly-owned off-shoot of the bank. It also provided export finance and leasing facilities. Perhaps, this decision to give factoring only divisional status, rather than elevate it —as National Westminster had done with Credit Factoring—to a more predominant position, reflected a view within Barclays that it represented just an addition to their range of services, rather than a major piece of diversification. But like Credit Factoring, B.E.A.F.C.O. places considerable emphasis on the non-financial aspects of factoring, such as the credit insurance and sales ledger accounting services.

Barclays Export Finance Company had been set up some seven years earlier to finance exports. It was originally owned jointly by Barclays Bank and Barclays D.C.O. (the old colonial bank which later became Barclays International). The Export Finance Company gave notice of its extended range of activities by the simple expedient of putting 'and' between the words 'Export' and 'Finance' in its name.

The factoring operation is essentially a 'without recourse, notification' service. Additionally an invoice discounting facility is provided. By early 1973 turnover (including invoice discounting) was running at between £5M and £6M. The B.E.A.F.C.O. factoring division had raised the number of its clients to ten, and employed a similar number of staff. In spite of the initial low profile, there are ambitious plans for the future, which envisage a turnover within five years of £70M (£50M for factoring and £20M for invoice discounting). An early penetration into export factoring was also planned. With Barclays International branches in many parts of the world, the B.E.A.F.C.O. factoring division has a very considerable advantage should it follow National Westminster's example and set up its own international network for conducting factoring on a global basis.

Goode Durrant & Murray

There are, in addition to these nine factoring houses, two other leading financers involved in kindred activities—Goode Durrant & Murray Ltd and London Bridge. Indeed, the former group claim to have invented the method of invoice discounting commonly practised in Britain today. It has the largest invoice discounting turnover of any house specializing in that kind of debt finance. G.D.M. Ltd itself is part of a pyramidal structure of companies organized within a publicly quoted holding company called Goode Durrant & Murray (Consolidated) and ultimately owned by Goode Durrant & Murray Group Ltd, whose other interests include retailing, leasing, hire purchase, shipping and forwarding, banking, confirming, and property financing.

Formed in the middle of the last century G.D.M. shares with Alex Lawrie the distinction of a colonial past. Originally an Australian warehousing company, it turned to confirming in the 1920s and expanded into other areas of financing in the late 1950s. It was able to undertake a programme of diversification with funds raised from selling the Australian warehousing interests. Invoice discounting was one of the first products of diversification.

Unlike the factoring houses, G.D.M. does not regularly reveal what its turnover is in trade debt financing. However, in 1968, a company statement disclosed a turnover of £10M. Although, subsequently, there was a considerable increase in the volume of its invoice discounting business reaching a peak of £22½M, this trend was reversed during 1972 when credit was generally plentiful, interest rates were falling and corporate demand for capital was at a low ebb. By the following year turnover was running at an annual rate of some £15M. Because invoice discounting is exclusively a financing facility—providing none of the other services offered by factoring—client demand more directly mirrors the course of the national economy. If there is competition for capital and corporate cash demands are high—either for stock investment or to meet short-term commitments—invoice discounting represents a useful source of funds. Conversely, when cheaper bank credit is available or there is little pressure on cash resources, the attractions of an invoice discounting facility are sharply diminished.

London Bridge Finance

London Bridge Finance is the second of the two debt financing houses which conduct an operation similar in broad concept to factoring, if different in many particulars. In fact, the London Bridge system is probably unique. With an annual turnover in 1973 of £60M, it was also nearly as large as the leading factor. It shares with one factor a common founding institution. This is the credit insurance broker, Credit Consultants Ltd., which, having contributed to the establishment of London Bridge Finance, later went on to help set up Keep Bros. (Trading Capital) and H. & H. Factors. In 1959, Credit Consultants approached the Guardian Assurance with the proposition to form a company to specialize in trade debt finance. At about this time, a Lloyds Bank subsidiary, Export Refinance Corporation, used a similar method of financing outstanding debts as that proposed for the new company except that it disclosed the agency arrangement. Guardian agreed to the proposal and the new company was christened after the ancient bridge across the Thames which was visible from Regis House at that time (but since transported to Arizona). However, Guardian would seem to have quickly become concerned about venturing out of its traditional field of activity and an interest in L.B.F. was offered to the merchant bank Philip Hill Higginson—which bought 75 per cent. Then in 1965 when Philip Hill merged with M. Samuel to form Hill Samuel, the balance of the shares were acquired and L.B.F. became a wholly owned subsidiary. Perhaps because in its early years insufficient resources were placed at its disposal, L.B.F. showed little growth between 1959 and 1965. But on receiving the full commitment of its new parent, turnover was expanded rapidly. It has a staff of only 15 and would barely need to increase this number by two or three people to conduct an £80M or £90M turnover. This is because unlike factoring, where the financing institution collects the debts and deals with the invoicing, the clients of L.B.F. continue to undertake these functions on its behalf; L.B.F. becomes the principal in the sale of its client's products, albeit a passive one.

As with invoice discounting, L.B.F. does not necessarily handle the entire turnover of its clients, but rather extends a facility that can be used when needed, supplying the volume of funds (up to agreed amounts) required at any given moment. Problems arose, however, during the months before the introduction of Valued Added Tax. As L.B.F. becomes the owner and principal in the sale of goods, it appeared that it was subject to V.A.T. on the transactions between itself and its agent, whereas the financial transactions of factors are exempt. If this ruling was strictly observed, the extra costs involved would have driven L.B.F. out of business. For a time no fresh clients were accepted and the L.B.F. management contemplated informing its existing clients that their facilities might have to be withdrawn. Fortunately, a sympathetic chord was struck at H.M. Customs and Excise which allowed a formula to be devised within the terms of the Finance Act enabling L.B.F. to continue operating and to sign up new business again.

7 Multinational Factoring

The greatest growth potential for factoring lies in the area of international trade. The constraints intermittently imposed by governments on the expansion of home economies, particularly those imposed upon Britain since the war by the exigencies of trade imbalances, diminish in importance when set in the context of a world-wide scale of operations. For the scope is widened by the existence of many foreign economies at different stages of the growth-recession cycle. At every stage in the evolution of factoring, its driving force has been its application to the international market.

Anglo-American trade was to the fore in the minds of the first transatlantic factors who explored the potential of Britain as a place to extend their activities. They believed that factoring techniques could facilitate the increasing exchange of goods between the two countries and provide assistance to both the experienced, and the uninitiated, exporter. 'Cracking' a new overseas market is often extraordinarily difficult. Frequently, the would-be exporter will not appreciate the special requirements, the local trade practices and the market fashions within the country to which he is attempting to sell. Cash against shipping documents, or letters of credit, are not the methods of settlement always readily accepted in a world where credit is customary and where the early post-war sellers' markets have been transformed into buyers' markets.

The aid of a factor who can arrange documentation—and in some cases finance the cost of import duties and internal delivery charges within the importing country—who can offer the buyer the credit terms normal in his trade, recommend marketing methods suited to each product, speak the language of the customer, and introduce the exporter to agents and distributors, can be invaluable. The growth of multinational factoring is largely the result of the explosion in world trade during the 1960s and the parallel drive towards the internationalization of banking (just as the old-style trade factor flourished with the expansion of the Roman Empire and the advent of the Medieval merchant-adventurer).

The dynamic forces released by the commercial integration of the European Community, together with the rise of industrial Japan and the industrialization of parts of Asia and Latin America, provide the ideal basis for a considerable development of multinational factoring.

Even the largest of European or American manufacturing companies can encounter problems when operating in unfamiliar territory. It is no coincidence that many of those clients served in foreign markets by a factor, are the exporting divisions of substantial companies, some of whom choose to have only their overseas business factored, being more than equal to the tasks of domestic sales accounting and collection. For, while the exporting company can only be exclusively responsible for the quality of its product, the factor can contribute to its competitiveness and to the simplification of the terms on which it is sold. Notwithstanding the factor's commission, his help may permit merchandise to be sold abroad more cheaply than it otherwise would, because the need to employ specialist import houses and obtain export financing facilities is eliminated. So, also, is the need to purchase forward foreign exchange 'cover' (to insure against changes in currency values) because the factor pays his client in sterling on immediate shipment of his goods.

It is for benefits such as these that the export divisions of Courtaulds, English Calico, Carrington Vyella and other equally well known British companies, have factored their overseas sales—and almost exclusively on a 'maturity' basis.

There are three multinational factoring networks and one voluntary international grouping of factoring houses. The latter was established with administering institutions to permit export-import business to be conducted between factors unconnected with one of the large multinationals. The future could also witness the formation of further overseas networks by American or British banks. At the centre of two of the existing multinationals are American factors. These are the First National Bank of Boston, the mid-wife of the International Factors Group, and the Walter E. Heller International Corporation, parent company of the Walter E. Heller Overseas Corporation, which controls its world-wide factoring operations.

The third of the multinational factors is the British-controlled Credit Factoring International, wholly owned by the National Westminster Bank.

Although inherently more specialized than the domestic operation, import-export factoring employs the same techniques and provides the same essential services. The work is shared between two factors—one in the importing country and one in the exporting country (except in the case of Credit Factoring which uses its own overseas offices). The importing factor is responsible for gleaning the credit information about the buyer and for collecting the payment, The exporting factor will conduct the sales accounting and advance cash on shipment of goods. If immediate cash is not required, the seller will be guaranteed payment within a fixed period related to normal credit terms. The seller receives 100 per cent indemnity against loss through bad debts up to the agreed credit limit whether the payment is made on 'open credit' terms or on bills of exchange. Protection is also often provided against customers' failure to pay for political reasons and against foreign exchange risks. In addition, the factor may provide general marketing assistance, sales statistics, customs clearance, direct delivery to the buyer and other ancillary services.

Overseas customers pay direct to the factor's account at a local bank or to the local factor himself. The import factor immediately transfers the remittance to the export factor. Thus, settlement is made with the minimum of delay. Disputes over the quality of the exporter's goods or general misunderstandings can be quickly dealt with by the local factor who is versed in the language and national custom and practice. Statements and payment reminders can similarly be dispatched in the language and format familiar to the importing customer. As a result, the normally complicated and time-consuming procedures involved in selling overseas, become little more difficult than selling to customers in the same town. The risks of non-payment and hazards of foreign currency transactions are sharply reduced. Payment is received promptly, so company liquidity is not strained by months of delay in the transmission of monies.

For example, let us suppose that the Italian agent of an English textile manufacturer secures an order to supply a fashion store in Milan with shirts. The agent will seek credit approval from the local factor for the approximate amount of the order. When this is received, the agent will send the order and the credit approval to the textile manufacturer. The latter will dispatch the shirts, raise the invoice in lire and offer credit terms appropriate for these goods in the Italian market. The manufacturer will send a copy of the invoice to the British factoring company (if it did not go direct to it in the first instance) and will receive payment in sterling, either immediately, or, should the exporter not need finance, on an agreed date.

This is comparatively straightforward, but let us take another case. Suppose a representative of a Hamburg company approached a Scottish manufacturer of electric organs. The German says his name is Herr Ertlemann and that he is the chief buyer for a firm of importers and suppliers of musical instruments called Brunsky, Ertlemann A. G. He places an order for 10 organs costing a total of £10,000. The organ maker promises delivery within two months and arranges the method of payment. He then contacts his factor, who in turn wires his opposite number in West Germany for credit approval, providing details of the buyer.

In 48 hours the German factor replies: 'Re: Brunsky, Ertlemann A.G., Hamburg. Name found to be fictitious. The address supplied found to be above empty warehouse. Premises also used for dubious shipping and freighter business. Last registered owner served three years in prison for fraud. Suggest cancel order.' The organ maker would appear to have been saved from making an expensive mistake. The credit check conducted by the German factor has revealed a very alarming set of circumstances. It is unlikely that the would-be exporter could have discovered these facts without assistance. Even if he spoke German fluently and had he gone personally to Hamburg, it would have been a time-consuming and, no doubt, very puzzling experience.

There are are other ways too, in which the overseas factor's knowledge of the local market can be of assistance. Let us take as a final example, a Sheffied cutlery producer who deals not with an agent, but through a specialist distributor. These specialists often elicit a very considerable 'mark up' on the price of the goods to the ultimate buyer, whom the seller rarely knows. As a consequence, the seller is obliged to retain the distributor no matter how unsatisfactory the arrangement, because if he parts company with him the ultimate customers will also be lost. In these circumstances, the local factor—perhaps with many other similar deals in hand—should be able to find new outlets within the same area.

The Networks

The internationalization of factoring was a natural development for the progressive American factoring houses used to dealing with companies separated by huge distances, establishing credit ratings for buyers across many states and making collections in areas demanding special local knowledge. It was not a big step when U.S. factors made agreements with large exporters in Japan to purchase their accounts receivables on their American customers. The formation of the European Free Trade Association and the European Economic Community was then contributing to the reduction of trade barriers like import restrictions and customs duties, opening the doors to more liberal trade and increased export competition. The Kennedy Round of multinational trade negotiations was similarly helping towards this end.

It was an obvious move to establish international factoring networks through which the differing administrative procedures of trading nations could be further ironed out. Through these networks overseas transactions could be better orchestrated, information disseminated and, with automatic data processing techniques, foreign business evaluated rapidly.

The four international factoring networks can, for convenience, be classed in two categories—the 'closed' networks of the multinationals numbering three, and the single 'open' network. Between them, these groups probably account for 90 per cent of all factoring conducted off the American mainland and most factoring houses outside of the U.S. belong to one or other or them.

Thanks to the extensive penetration of factoring during the past ten years, much of the globe is now covered by the factoring networks, including all of Western Europe, North America, parts of South America, areas of the Caribbean, the more industrialized parts of Asia, Australasia, the Middle East, and South Africa. Indeed, the only countries in which factoring is sparsely represented are those with less developed economies or centrally planned economies. There have even been attempts since the easing of political tension in Europe, to extend factoring to the Soviet Union and other Eastern bloc countries.

The 'closed' networks—International Factors Group, the Walter E. Heller Overseas Corporation and Credit Factoring International—constitute the groups of factors bound by some kind of direct financial link—either subsidiaries, branch offices, or affiliated companies—with a common shareholder or (in the case of Credit Factoring International) a central administrative and clearing centre. Members of these networks deal solely through their sister factors or own offices within the network. In the case of the Heller and I.F.G., the many sister companies comprise joint enterprises between the multinational company and local financial institutions (such as H. & H. Factors in Britain, owned by Hambros Bank and Heller; and International Factors Ltd, owned by First National Bank of Boston and Lloyds and Scottish Finance).

In contrast, Credit Factoring International established its own offices in several countries, and only subsequently permitted some selected local participation in their operations. Credit Factoring has the advantage of a centralized computer system and administration, but, equally, can sometimes lack the more comprehensive information-gathering capabilities and broad base that fuller local participation can contribute. Local participation has been sought as Credit Factoring International began to develop beyond a preoccupation with outgoing trade from Britain, to a more multi-directional system, including trade between third countries. It is therefore even more homogeneous than the other two 'closed' networks where the greater diffusion of ownership lends a more distinctive local character to the factor's operations.

Factors Chain International represents the only 'open' network. This means that almost any factoring house can become a member so long as the ultimate ownership is of high standing. All members are in open competition with each other and there is frequently more than one F.C.I. member in each country. For example, there are four members of F.C.I. in the U.S., and in Sweden. In West Germany there are five members of the chain. There were also five British members at one time, but mergers reduced the number to two. In spite of a genuine need for such a chain, it is probably the case that its development received impetus from the steady formation of the other networks; and the motive was primarily the desire of the non-aligned factors to offer competitive international services. The principal qualification for a factor joining the F.C.I. is that it can display solid backing from banks, insurance company or other major financial institution. This is necessary so that other members of the chain can have confidence that in the event of losses being sustained on an international transaction, the correspondent factor can meet his obligations. A secretariat in Amsterdam provides the basic organizational framework.

International Factors Group

The International Factors Group had a world-wide turnover of some $2,000M in 1973. Of this, the domestic American operation of First National Bank of Boston accounted for roughly half. It covers 23 countries, the last to be established being in Japan when Orient Factors was set up in November 1972, with an initial paid-in capital of $1·2M. Japan has been a difficult market for factoring to get a foothold because so much of the nation's commerce is conducted by the huge industrial corporations, particularly the overseas trade. These corporations handle much of the foreign business of even the smaller Japanese companies. International Factors became the first factor to enter the Japanese market (although New York factors had previously collected accounts receivables arising from Japanese sales to America). Until the I.F.G. added Orient Factors to its list of affiliated companies, the absence of Japanese representation was a glaring omission in the geographical spread of factoring.

In keeping with the established pattern of the International Factors Group, Orient Factors was a joint exercise between the First National

Bank of Boston and important local institutions. In this case these were the Sanwa Bank of Osaka (Japan's fifth largest bank with deposits of some $12,500M), Tokyo Trust and Banking Co., Nissho Iwai Co., Nichiment Co., and Orient Leasing Co. The new factor was intended to facilitate both domestic Japanese and international business and was set up with a particular eye to the predicted rise in British exports to Japan. Indeed, it was International Factors of Britain, rather than the International Factors Group, that was primatily responsible for the formation of the Orient offshoot.

I.F.G. has a geographical spread virtually as wide as any of the networks, but the list is not definitive. India and Pakistan are beginning to offer factoring possibilities as they industrialize, while parts of Latin America might also profitably be added to the global coverage. It was I.F.G. that first tentatively approached the U.S.S.R. to explore the possibility of factoring East-West trade. However, this proved an impractical proposition at the time.

The First National Bank's shareholdings in the I.F.G. members varies from between 5 and 25 per cent normally, although in one exceptional case, the stake is 33 per cent. In the early days of International Factor's geographical expansion, First National Bank founded a Swiss umbrella company to co-ordinate its many interests in overseas enterprises. This umbrella company was called International Factors A.G. (I.F.A.G.). The various other institutions throughout the world which participated in these enterprises also had stakes in I.F.A.G. through a complicated series of cross-shareholdings. I.F.A.G., in turn had share interests in the many satellite factoring companies. But this system of ownership was found to have a restrictive effect, in some cases retarding the development of a local factor when it wished to raise finance. Consequently, the arrangement was unwound and individual shareholdings were bought back from I.F.A.G. by the local participant institutions.

The resulting loose arrangement within the network threatened problems in co-ordinating group systems and practices. To counter this, the International Factors Group set up in June 1974 an international co-ordinating office in Brussels to iron out difficulties between the member companies and direct the harmonization programmes. This office is intended not only to ensure that group operating standards are uniform in each country, but also to promote export–import factoring and develop new markets.

In addition, there is a permanent finance committee, an advertizing and public relations committee and others which deal with standardization and exchange of information, compatibility of computer systems and further items of common interest. *Ad hoc* committees are also formed to examine work-a-day problems as they arise. Forty or fifty of the chief executives of the group companies meet once a year in September for four or five days. A different location is chosen for this meeting each time. To this annual meeting the various committees report and make their recommendations. The conference also allows the many chief executives to establish closer contact and create a more intimate relationship. The working language is English.

All of these activities help to weld a relatively loosely organized group into a coherent force and provide a sense of identity. For a similar purpose a common logo is used throughout the network. Moreover, there is an Inter-Factor Agreement, under which the I.F.G. members undertake to use uniform communication systems, follow common regulations and procedures, and look after the best interests of their counterparts within the group. It also provides for a specific scale of charges in an attempt to minimize the inevitable double overheads and the consequential need for high commissions in export-import business. Every phase of the international operation has an agreed charge, paid to whichever factor carries out the particular leg of a transaction.

In this way, the charge for factoring exports and imports may not be materially greater than for domestic business. The differences can be much less than 0·5 percentage point. In some cases it may be even as little as 0·05 per cent. Where the client has both domestic and overseas factored, the cost of the latter may be subsumed within an overall fee. This is notwithstanding the fact that the overseas sister company, backed by many of the largest institutions in that country, may be making credit assessments which could not possibly be made from Britain, especially for those places where credit information is anyway rudimentary; and furthermore, it might be making a speedy collection of monies, for which the exporter might otherwise have had to wait many months.

Walter E. Heller

Many of the I.F.G. concepts are shared by the Walter E. Heller network. Heller is represented in 21 countries, and commanded a total factoring turnover of $1,800M in 1973, of which some $525M represented operations outside the U.S. It is by far the largest factor in America and much of its turnover is derived from that very large market. But the operations of European subsidiaries are expanding rapidly, particularly in the international field. Some 40 per cent of the business conducted by its Dutch offshoot is in export-import factoring, while in West Germany the Heller company gains half of its turnover from international trade. For Italy, the figure is around

45 per cent, but in Britain H. & H. Factors' foreign trade is a comparatively modest 25 per cent of total.

The Structure of the Walter E. Heller International Corporation comprises three main operating divisions. These are Walter E. Heller & Company, which accounts for all the domestic American financial operations including factoring, leasing, accounts receivable financing, consumer credit, computer time sharing and real estate finance; Walter E. Heller Industries, Inc., the manufacturing division; and Walter E. Heller Overseas Corporation, which controls the overseas factoring network.

The entire organization is huge—the total volume of business handled by the finance and overseas divisions alone reached $6,500M in 1973. The overseas factors in the group operate on a semi-autonomous basis. With the exception of West Germany, the financial institutions who participate in the various Heller factoring companies around the world usually own just less than 50 per cent of the equity, providing Heller with the controlling interest. In the case of Canada, Puerto Rico and Jamaica, no local company has been established, and Heller has chosen instead to service these markets through branch offices of the main American company. In three other countries, it has only a comparatively modest stake in the local affiliated member of the network.

The latest two countries in which Heller has hoisted its flag are Hong Kong and Israel. A Hong Kong factor was set up in partnership with Jardine, Matheson & Company, the British merchant house, and the Bank of East Asia. Both have their headquarters in the colony and each owns 30 per cent in the new enterprise; Heller owns the remaining 40 per cent. The choice of Hong Kong as a location for a further extension of the network exemplifies the trend towards the development of factoring in the Pacific Basin. The colony's role as a major exporter of finished goods, particulary textiles, and its reliance on outside supplies of raw materials, create an ideal environment for factoring to take root. At the same time, the desire for solid partners in such enterprise is apparent. The 130-year old company of Jardine, Matheson pre-dates the founding of Hong Kong as a British colony, while the Bank of East Asia is owned by Chinese Hong Kong nationals and is one of the major Chinese-owned banks in the Orient, with branches throughout the Far East, including Mainland China.

A little earlier than the Hong Kong enterprise came Walter E. Heller Israel Ltd, established in Tel Aviv. This venture—45 per cent owned by Heller—has drawn the participation of C.L.A.L. Israel Investment Co., the largest general investment company in the country, and a 10 per cent from Israel Sacharov and Company, a private local investment firm. C.L.A.L. itself is half-owned by the three largest Israeli banks. Since its inception, the new company has been increasingly active in factoring on behalf of diamond exporters, producers of textiles and citrus fruits, and other industries.

The Hong Kong and Israel enterprises represent early steps in the transmission of factoring to developing economies. But the Heller group also seem to have achieved the first factoring arrangement with an Eastern Bloc country. In the summer of 1972, executives of Heller Factoring Bank A.G., of Mainz, West Germany, entered into an agreement with Hungarotex, the Hungarian government sales agency representing that nation's 200 textile mills. These have a combined annual volume estimated at more than $300M. The arrangement provides for 'maturity' factoring of Hungarian textile exports through Heller's international network, enabling the nation's mills to sell on an open account basis throughout the Western world. This agreement was followed by a second, and similar scheme, with Chemolimpex, the export agency for Hungary's chemical industry. Other such agreements are likely to follow in the future. Communist countries and developing countries offer considerable scope for the further extension of international factoring.

For both types of economy foreign markets are becoming increasingly important for earning foreign exchange with which to purchase the necessary goods and machinery for their development. But in many cases they are broaching European and North American markets with little experience upon which to draw and no traditional patterns for marketing, selling and settling debts exists for them.

Heller's first overseas factoring subsidiaries were in Britain and West Germany in 1964. However, the German operation was set up without local bank support and this was soon seen to have been a mistake. Heller then changed tactics and invited local participation in its scheme, and this established the pattern for most later enterprises.

Heller's preference for a majority shareholding in its satellites provides for inherently greater central control within the network than might be the case of the rival International Factors Group system. But it also finds it useful to hold annual conferences of group chief executives. It additionally has an inter-group agreement covering procedures, standards and the scaling and division of export-import commissions.

Like I.F.G. the Heller group employs *ad hoc* committees to iron out problems that arise between members, having a co-ordinating office in Utrecht which seeks to harmonize and orchestrate international operations. One potential source of dislocation is the variety of computer systems used by various sister companies, which generate compatibility problems. Commissions on international transactions

COUNTRIES COVERED BY THE MULTINATIONAL FACTORING NETWORKS

International Factors Group	*Heller Overseas Corporation*	*Factors Chain International*	*Credit Factoring International*
Austria	Argentina	Austria	Austria
Australia	Australia	Belgium	Belgium
Belgium	Belgium	Canada	Canada
Denmark	Canada	Denmark	Denmark
Finland	Denmark	Finland	Finland
France	France	France	France
Holland	Holland	Holland	Holland
Israel	Hong Kong	Israel	Hong Kong
Italy	Israel	Italy	Italy
Japan	Italy	Norway	Republic of Ireland
New Zealand	Jamaica	Republic of Ireland	Singapore
Norway	Mexico	South Africa	Sweden
Republic of Ireland	Norway	Spain	Switzerland
Portugal	Philippines	Sweden	United Kingdom
South Africa	Portugal	Switzerland	United States
Spain	Puerto Rico	United Kingdom	West Germany
Sweden	South Africa	United States	Norway
Switzerland	Spain	West Germany	
United Kingdom	Sweden		
United States	United Kingdom		
West Germany	United States		
	West Germany		

through the Heller group can cost up to ½ percentage point more than for the simpler domestic business, but as the average invoice sums tend to be higher on export-import trade, some of the extra cost incurred can frequently be absorbed by the factors themselves. Even so, because of the extra resources necessarily deployed in foreign transactions, Heller has found, in common with the other networks, that only a streamlined and smooth operation can keep the cost to the client down to acceptable levels.

Factors Chain International

The genesis of the Factors Chain International was a co-operation agreement between Shield Factors of Britain and Svensk Factoring A.B. of Sweden, signed in Stockholm in 1964. This initial agreement was developed into a larger organization when Factors Chain was formed in Stockholm in the spring of the following year. Besides Svensk and Shield, the other founding members were S/S Factoring, Oslo; Factoring-rahoitus Oy, Helsinki and Forenede Factors A/S, Copenhagen. Hubshman Factors, a division of First National City

Bank of New York, joined the chain as an associate member. But the most important development for the 'open' chain concept occurred in 1968 when at a meeting in Baden-Baden, delegates from 14 factoring companies in eleven countries decided to extend the scope of the chain by the formation of a truly world-wide service network.

A committee was appointed to work out the plans for the chain's reorganization, providing for substantially increased activity. Five months later, these preparations culminated in a conference attended by executives from 30 factoring houses in 15 countries. This conference gave birth to Factors Chain International.

The F.C.I. declared that its aims would be: to increase factoring co-operation across national boundaries; to develop uniform factoring techniques; and to help in solving legal and technical problems in international factoring and other problems directly or indirectly appertaining to factoring in general.

A permanent four-man secretariat was established in Amsterdam, historically the capital of factoring in the 17th and 18th centuries. By 1973, the F.C.I. boasted some 35 members in 18 countries. Its total factored turnover was estimated to have been around $5,800M in 1972—making it the largest of the international networks. However, much more than half of this turnover was attributable to the American members, Talcott Factors, William Iselin & Co., Dommerich (a Chemical Bank subsidiary), and the factoring division of the First National City Bank of New York.

Under the F.C.I. constitution, it has a council on which sit representatives from each member. This is the highest decision-making body within the organization. Amongst its duties is the appointment of individuals to the Executive Committee. This has ten members, some of whom alternate, plus a chairman and vice-chairman. Half the committee members have a vote, while others contribute to discussions as experienced factors.

There are full annual meetings of the council, and the Executive Committee meets four or five times a year. In addition, there are regular F.C.I. educational seminars. In spite of its elaborate constitution, the 'chain' probably tends to suffer—because of its nature and size—from greater difficulties of co-ordination and collaboration than the more homogenous networks. Delays in the transmitting of credit assessments and remittance of customer payments, together with inevitable problems over the division of commissions, have both necessitated remedial action and intensified the drive to create from the disparate parts of the F.C.I. a coherent and competitive force in international factoring.

Yet, at the same time, many of the smaller factoring houses appear to be only passive members of the 'chain'; not all the members have shown the same degree of fidelity to the group or identified with it fully. But, notwithstanding the organizational limitations of an association formed from voluntary participation by independent companies, a large proportion of those unaligned factors outside of the U.S. have seen fit to join the F.C.I. Most of those that have not joined are the relatively small factors with little desire to involve themselves in areas outside their home markets. Membership of the F.C.I. requires a heavy annual fee and the factors' willingness to pay provides some proof of the group's value to the individual members. The annual fee is actually decided in the light of the budget for the year.

Such measures as the F.C.I. uniform code of communications have helped to reduce problems within the organization. The manual governing communication procedures was drawn up by one of its committees, of which there are four, each manned by 8 to 10 people, and covering, in addition to communications, areas like standardization, legal aspects, public relations and marketing. There have been a number of efforts to eliminate the costs of double handling. Normally, the bulk of the commission goes to the factor handling the imports as he does most of the work. Ideally, a client with a large percentage of exports within his total turnover, should find himself paying only marginally more when using the F.C.I. correspondent network than for domestic factoring alone. But the cost could rise for comparatively small export totals. A minimum annual volume equivalent to $100,000 to $200,000 is frequently required for clients exclusively using the export service.

The F.C.I. secretariat tackles the day-to-day problems that arise, attempting to resolve disagreements and identify potential areas of discord. The formal objectives of the secretariat are to further the development of factoring and to function as a point of contact and source of information for members, authorities and organizations.

The cause of international factoring has not only been advanced by such expressions of the collective spirit as F.C.I., but also by the initiative of individual members. Svensk Factoring (one of the F.C.I. founding members) introduced in 1968 the first complete package of services for small and medium-sized exporters. The package consisted of normal export factoring, with credit advances and accounts receivable book-keeping, together with forwarding and freight brokerage facilities. The entire package was calculated to provide an exporter with door-to-door service. It was arranged in conjunction with a specialist company in transport, freight brokerage and forwarding. For the small unsophisticated manufacturer, unused to trading in foreign markets, so fraught with hidden problems, the task could at last become simpler than selling within the producer's own neighbourhood.

Credit Factoring

Of all the networks, Credit Factoring International is by far the most centrally controlled and administered. All transactions are channelled through the computer clearing system in Feltham, Middlesex. There is a clearly defined common discipline for the group, standard accounting and managerial practices, and centralized market research and problem-solving units. Credit Factoring has 14 overseas offices covering 17 countries, effectively extending across most of Western Europe and including the Far East and the U.S. But some of these offices serve only British exports and do not conduct local domestic factoring within these countries, although this single-purpose structure is gradually being broadened. However, there is to be no dilution of the central clearing house concept. It is envisaged that partnerships like those forged in Italy, Singapore, Hong Kong and the U.S., will result ultimately in a more thoroughly multi-directional system, but emphasis will remain on international trade. Initially a member of Factors Chain International, Credit Factoring pertinaciously concluded that only a system of its own design and under its own control would provide the necessary framework for an ambitious extension of its overseas activities. Although still the smallest of multinational networks, its decision to 'go it alone' could prove to be of considerable significance for international factoring if the course it is charting were followed by other currently unaligned companies.

Credit Factoring's overseas branches are staffed and run by nationals of the local country, but all personnel are specially trained to operate the one uniform system. Branch routines, procedures and administration are spelt out in a basic manual. There are three-month full-time courses for foreign staff. They learn that all debts are logged on customer accounts in the currencies in which goods are sold, but that simultaneously the computer will convert these foreign currencies to sterling at the day's 'spot' exchange rate. When the sterling balance has been established it is credited to the client. Trainees will also be informed that the computer is programmed to instruct the customer to make payments to the local Credit Factoring branch office, that all money is then remitted to the British office, and that, if necessary, reminder letters in the customers' own language are sent from Feltham to the overseas branches for signing and posting. In this way a rigid discipline is imposed on the whole group. Turnover of the international business is still comparatively small, running at rather less than £20M at the beginning of 1974.

Factoring and World Trade

In spite of the growth of export-import factoring, its importance in in world trade is still relatively modest in the context of total exports of the non-communist areas, which in 1972 amounted to some $372,000M. The increasing interdependence of the developed world has led to an unprecedented expansion in trade. In the last decade the value of exports has more than tripled, and by 1980 it is predicted to reach $500,000M. In contrast, total factoring throughout the world is probably approaching $20,000M (excluding $26,000M of American receivables financing), and only a small portion of this represents export-import factoring, as opposed to domestic factoring. Although the U.S. accounts for more than three-quarters of all the factoring which takes place on the globe, the volume of that country's exported merchandise actually handled by its factors is tiny. This is in spite of the high hopes of those pioneers within the industry who, at the beginning of the 1960s, founded British subsidiaries to facilitate Anglo-American trade. Yet this lack of success probably reflects the relative unimportance of exports and imports in the American economy. In Europe, where foreign trade plays a more important role, up to 20 per cent of the total $3,000M of factored business may be passing between nations. The proportion is growing rapidly, and with the continued sharp expansion of international trade expected during the rest of this decade, factoring should play an increasingly important part in that expansion.

For inevitably this growth in trade will have to be accompanied by an equivalent increase both in the means of settling international transactions and in the credit that is needed to facilitate such an upsurge in commerce. The British situation exemplifies the desirability of these simultaneous developments. In 1960, the United Kingdom exported goods to the value of £3,732M, or £311M a month, on average. By 1973, there had been a huge rise—exports were running at about £12,000M a year, or £1,000M a month. Much of this was of necessity being financed by the banks. Few of the major industrial companies will have anything like the spare liquidity needed to sustain the level and value of trade debts suggested by trade of this magnitude.

As a result, there has in recent years, been a considerable widening and extension of the bank schemes for providing both export finance and pre-shipment finance. But, such borrowing increases costs, adding to an exporter's outlays, which may not be recoverable in a competitive market. Only a rapid transmission of funds between centres will reduce the exporter's bank charges. For this, together with speedier collection techniques specifically accelerates the conversion of manufactured products into cash.

The ultimate objective must be to reduce the settlement period on overseas transactions, at least to levels comparable with those for domestic sales. Frequently, at the moment, exporters have to wait much longer for foreign customers to pay for their purchases. For this reason alone, selling overseas can be far more onerous than selling in the home market; either liquidity problems are intensified or the cost of financing the operation mounts significantly. Yet, the competitive international market often demands not only attractive credit terms, but allows little scope for recouping the consequent financing costs through increased prices.

Regular surveys conducted by the Department of Trade and Industry reveal the kind of credit terms which exporters are obliged to provide. These suggest that some 56 per cent of exports are originally offered 'for cash or credit of up to 60 days' (how long actual settlements take is not known). In contrast, available evidence for credit on *domestic* transactions, indicates that some 75 per cent of sales are made on monthly settlement terms. Again, roughly a third of all exports are originally offered on credit terms ranging from 61 to 180 days (thus, nearly 90 per cent of exports are made on terms of six months or less), while 95 per cent of all home sales are initially made on credit terms of six weeks or less. It must be stressed that the Department of Trade and Industry surveys only take account of the 'original terms on which exports are made', not the time actual taken to pay, which may be much greater.

Amongst the industries within which relatively long credit terms are common on overseas sales are those in the chemical, engineering, paper, printing and publishing, rubber and distribution sectors. All of these receive a large proportion of their payments between 61 and 180 days after delivery. Two of Britain's largest exporting industries—the motor vehicle and non-electrical engineering industries—receive, respectively, 29 per cent and 32 per cent of all payments between 61 and 180 days after delivery. For food, drink and tobacco, and textiles, clothing and footwear, the proportion of remittances falling into this settlement bracket amounts to about a quarter of the total.

The only comfort in all this for exporters is that there does not appear to be any serious deterioration in the situation. During recent years there has been only a marginal—if steady—worsening of international credit terms. The slight worsening in fact, partly reflects the expansion of capital exports, which now account for about 40 per cent of exports. These are often on credit terms of more than a year, but are, in any case, unsuited to techniques like factoring.

For consumer goods, however, factoring can effectively constitute a cash sale at the time of shipment. Of course, a factor's advance represents a form of financing which has to be paid for like any other, but the integrated services of collection and credit underwriting, ensure speedier, easier and more secure settlement, keeping costs down. It also facilitates the use of the 'open account' method of settle-

INTERNATIONAL CREDIT TERMS

Original terms on which British exports were made	*Percentage of total exports* 1968	1969	1970	1971
Cash or credit of up to 60 days	57·8	57·5	56·6	55·7
Credit of 61 to 180 days	30·2	31·0	32·0	32·4
Credit of 181 days to 1 year	4·7	4·6	4·1	4·9
Credit of over 1 year and up to 21 months (*a*)	2·4	2·2	1·3	1·1
Credit of over 21 months and up to 5 years (*b*)	1·7	1·6	2·5	2·7
Credit of over 5 years	3·3	3·1	2·8	3·2
Total	100	100	100	100

(*a*) Credit of over 1 year and up to 3 years for 1968 and 1969.
(*b*) Credit of over 3 years and up to 5 years for 1968 and 1969.
Source: Department of Trade and Industry survey covering more than 1,500 companies.

ment, which can make international transactions nearly as simple as domestic business and, as a consequence, now represents the most popular means of paying for goods purchased. It is expected to become easily the most common method of payment for intra-E.E.C. trade, and already accounts for 60 per cent of all cross-frontier Community business (and perhaps 40 to 50 per cent of all international trade).

But, there is a further element in international settlement, as well as speed and ease of payment—that of foreign exchange. For the British exporter or importer, receiving, or making, payment in sterling, this does not arise. But with the gradual decline in the importance of the pound as a trading currency, the purchase and sale of foreign currencies on the exchange markets has become a necessary part of trading overseas. This has not been made easier by the continued bouts of currency speculation and the increasingly more frequent adjustments in exchange rate parities. The regime of universal floating exchange rates which was introduced in the spring of 1973 has spotlighted this problem. A rise or fall of a few points in one currency against another can quickly eliminate a profit on a foreign sale, perhaps turning it into a loss. Insuring against exchange rate movements by purchasing or selling currencies in the forward markets can be expensive.

Yet since sterling's 14 per cent devaluation in November 1967, the number of exchange rate changes has been prodigious. On 21 December 1971, there was a complete realignment of the major currencies. But, between that date and the Autumn of 1973, sterling had suffered an effective devaluation against other key currencies of nearly 20 per cent. (This calculation is weighted to allow for the proportion of trade transacted between Britain and its most important trading partners.) Over a similar period, the Italian lira and United States dollar had been, on the same basis, devalued by nearly 11 per cent. At the same time, the Deutschemark, the Japanese yen, Netherlands guilder and the Swiss, French and Belgium francs had been revalued by 18½ per cent, 10 per cent, 5 per cent, 14 per cent, 4 per cent, and 3 per cent respectively. Exchange rate movements between individual currencies were often even greater than suggested by these weighted overall changes. The Deutschemark increased in value by about 40 per cent against the Dollar in the first seven months of 1973 and fell by 20 per cent in the last five months of that year. Such large and numerous exchange rate revisions cannot have failed to affect the trading patterns of many companies, although some will have made profits from currency movements. The immediate advance of funds in sterling by a factor completely eliminates the threat posed to the exporter by such exchange rate movements. The finance director of an exporting company no longer has to worry about 'covering forward', or spending hours studying the form of other nations' economies, making certain his company's affairs are so arranged to minimize the effects of any adverse currency movements . The larger exporter no doubt gains on the swings what it loses on the roundabouts, but the smaller company is more exposed to dangers presented by unstable exchange rates. Allowance for exchange rate movements cannot be made when budgeting and their effects cannot be quantified in advance. The risks can be considerable, maybe threatening company profitability while the gratuitous profits from such movements are no more than a bonus. It is a risk which the factor, with his greater aggregate turnover, is better placed to provide for.

8 *Factoring in the Main Industrial Countries*

The importance of factoring and receivables financing as a source of funds for some sectors of United States industry has been substantial. In recent years, factoring has grown steadily in America, broadly in line with the expansion in the country's gross national product. Throughout the 1950s and 1960s, aggregate turnover of U.S. factoring houses amounted to about roughly 1 per cent of the G.N.P. But more recently, factoring has grown faster than the national economy, and in 1972 stood at 1·3 per cent of G.N.P. If factoring and receivables financing are taken together, the percentage rises to more than 3½ per cent. The American economy is so huge and infinitely adaptive that the actual overall effect of these forms of financing is unquantifiable—if factoring did not exist some other techniques would no doubt have evolved for similar purposes. What is clear is that whole industries in fact owe their development to the existence of the factor. Between the wars, factoring became an economic force again in American commercial life because a need arose for the very special skills which it offered.

The rapid increase in U.S. factoring business testifies to this. It has grown from a mere $1,500M in 1944 to over $16,000M in 1973—an increase of nearly 1,000 per cent. Over the same period, business handled by receivables financing companies has expanded by something close to 2,000 per cent, passing the $20,000M mark around 1970 (compared with just $1,200M after the war).

In fact, receivables financing overtook factoring, in the value of business handled, in 1955, and until the large commercial banks began to enter the factoring field in the mid-1960s, it steadily widened its lead. Factoring did not grow very rapidly initially, taking nearly a quarter century to rise from a turnover of $790M to $5,500M in 1963, but has

THE COMPARATIVE TURNOVER OF U.S. FACTORS
($ million)

Company	1973	1972	1971	1970	1969
Ambassador (Industrial Natl. Bank)	185	170	140	127	111
A. J. Armstrong	280	235	175	130	110
H. A. Caesar (First Natl. Union Bancorp)	80	85	78	62	60
Century Factors	320	320	275	275	230
Chase Manhattan Bank	625	650	630	600	500
Citicorp Factors (First Natl. City)	580	525	475	400	310
Citizens & Southern Natl. Bank	592	464	309	203	162
Coleman Factors (Bankers Trust)	365	300	275	250	220
Congress Factors (Phila. Natl. Bank)	280	210	180	165	140
Dommerich (Chemical Bank)	385	835	748	613	403
First Pennsylvania Bank	215	165	105	54	27
FNB Financial (First Natl. Bank Boston)*	1,030	950	900	850	860
Walter E. Heller*	1,812	1,401	1,218	1,010	894
William Iselin	850	825	770	670	700
John P. Maguire (Provident Natl. Bank)	755	665	625	565	660
Manufacturers Hanover Commercial	505	445	400	425	390
Meinhard Commercial	1,175	1,075	1,045	1,010	1,015
Melberg Factors	260	215	185	150	125
NCNB Financial (North Carolina Natl. Bank)	160	140	88	65	40
Rawleigh Moses (Central Natl. Bank)	72	62	41	36	33
Rosenthal & Rosenthal	315	275	250	235	235
Rusch (Va. Commonwealth Bankshares)	245	190	110	85	80
Southeastern Financial (S)	630	550	360	295	293
Standard Factors	185	179	131	125	95
Sterling National Bank	85	75	60	—	8
James Talcott Factors	1,010	1,070	1,240	1,200	1,225
Textile Banking	580	540	610	575	575
Trust Co. of Georgia	375	325	275	270	290
United Factors	1,355	1,235	1,100	885	812
United Virginia Factors	445	445	493	473	430

*FNB Financial's figures do not include First Boston's minority interest in foreign factoring operations which totalled about $1.01 billion last year and some $1 billion in 1972. Heller's figures include foreign factoring estimated at more than $525 million in 1973 and about $305 million in 1972.

(S) Southeastern Financial is part of American Credit, whose acquisition by Wachovia Corp., holding company for Wachovia National Bank is being challenged (1973) in an antitrust action.

since accelerated dramatically. The more aggressive tactics employed by the American banks and the huge resources which they were able to mobilize in support of their factoring programmes, are chiefly responsible for this expansion.

Although the general interest of the banks in factoring is comparatively recent, by the end of 1973 nearly 50 per cent of all American factoring business was undertaken by divisions or subsidiaries of banks. This compares with bank participation in the industry of only 15·5 per cent in 1966.

These developments in the American factoring industry have their parallels in receivables financing, where turnover also rose very sharply in the 1960s, having climbed from a mere $411M in 1940. It had

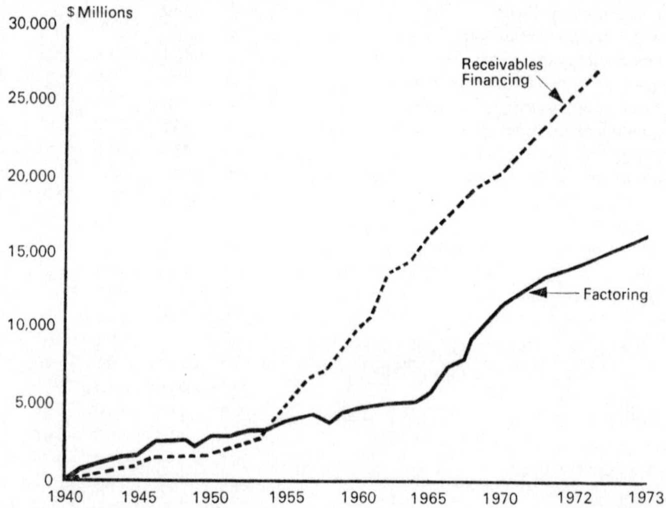

Figure 16. The growth of factoring and receivables financing in the U.S.

reached only $5,000M by 1956. At the same time, there has been an increasing trend for much of the receivables financing business to be concentrated in the hands of the larger commercial finance companies, some of which also conduct factoring operations. A little more than two dozen factors and commercial finance companies account for over two-thirds of total business in the two sectors together, whereas in 1966, these same companies represented only 58 per cent of the total.

Conceivably, the expansion of factoring would have been even faster than it has been, but for the continuing strong concentration in textiles and allied fields like furniture and shoes. Notwithstanding the diversification that has taken place, more than four-fifths of turnover is still derived from these sectors, with the greater part coming from textiles alone. The balance of the turnover, however, covers a wide spectrum, from electronics to poultry farming. In many ways, tradition seems still to tie the factor. He still appears most comfortable dealing with those industries for which he has built up a large body of information and for which he has a 'feel'. Constructing a comparable credit-assessing capacity in other sectors has proved no easy task.

The Position of Factoring in America today

American bank participation in factoring really stems from 1946 when the First National Bank of Boston (later the initiator of the International Factors network) was drawn into the field—leading most of its bank competitors by 20 years. But there were isolated, and more minor incursions into factoring by the banks during the 1930s. Both the Bank of America and the Trust Company of Georgia were involved in some form before the Second World War.

The First National Bank of Boston's venture into factoring sprang rather naturally from its considerable connections with the textile industry, having been set up in 1784 in New England, the cradle of textile manufacture. During the depression of the 1930s, as mills sought funds, or went broke, First National began to consider factoring its mill customers as a method of providing them with more working capital. But, it did not truly move in this direction until after the war.

The headlong stampede by the banks to purchase independent factoring houses actually began in the mid-1960s with the New York banks. The First National City Bank of New York's purchase of a factor called Hubshman led a list of factoring house takeovers which included the purchase of Dommerich by the Chemical Bank; Shapiro Factors by the Chase Manhattan Bank; and Coleman & Company by Bankers Trust. Between 1965 and 1968 some eight banks—mostly the larger and more energetic of their number—bought stakes in factoring houses. The trend was still apparent in 1971 and 1972. John P. Maguire and Co., and Ambassador Factors were acquired, respectively, by the Provident National Bank of Philadelphia and the Industrial National Bank, Providence, in 1971; Iselin-Jefferson Factors and Crompton-Richmond Co. Factors were bought respectively, by Manufacturers Hanover Trust and United Virginia, during 1972.

The floodgates were really opened in June 1963, when the then Comptroller of the currency, James Saxon, ruled that factoring was a proper area for national bank expansion. Until then, the factoring industry consisted of two dozen small and medium-sized houses and a few giant concerns. The banks' interest was two-fold. The first was simply the opportunity it presented to increase their profits, since interest rates of factors' advances are higher than for other forms of lending. The second reason was the desire to utilize more fully the computer hardware and ample manpower in which the banks had been competitively investing. The only obstacle to the banks' planned expansion of factoring, was the lack of trained personnel to handle a sharp increase in volume.

These concrete reasons for the bank expansion into factoring were set against a climate of more imaginative and sophisticated banking and an increasing need for experiment to cope with society's changing requirements. In their drive to meet all the financial needs of their customers, many of the more aggressive big city banks had already moved into fresh pastures, offering credit cards and accounting services. Some banks had already ventured into the more high-risk

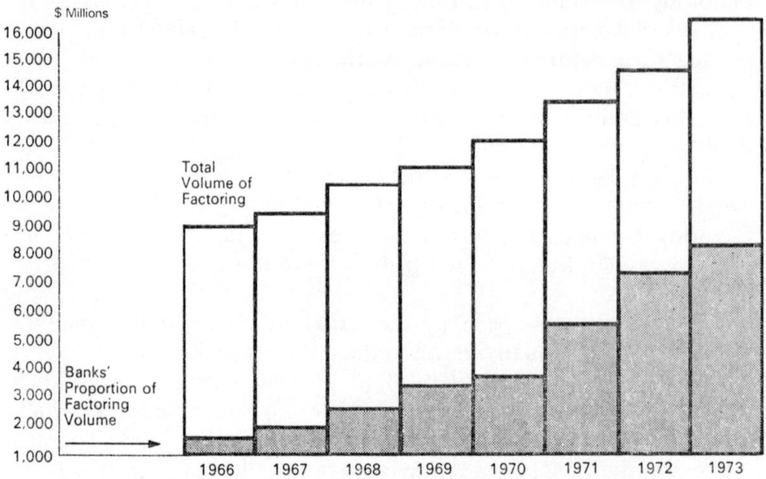

Figure 17. The banks' rising share of American factoring.

business of accounts receivable financing and lending against inventories or real estate. As part of this same expansion syndrome, they branched out into factoring. In many ways it was a logical extension of the development towards high-risk lending which in some cases had been apparent since the 1920s.

But, it is true, also, that many of the banks most attracted to factoring were located in, or involved with, areas of substantial textile, or allied industry interests, where old-line factoring was already an established and accepted force. Factoring was also attractive because it was a relatively stable business. The volume typically grew moderately from year to year and clients tended to remain with a factor for eight or nine years. By contrast, the average client turnover in receivable financing tended to be two or three years. Consistent with the higher risk, the rates of profit return on factoring were greater than for some other bank activities. Moreover, banks also obtained their own funds at a lower cost than non-bank factors because they did not depend solely on the money and capital markets, but could solicit for deposits. Finally, the ability of large city banks to offer factoring services to their correspondent banks in other parts of the country was a further advantage of their interest in this area. Yet the banks' involvement was not without its benefits to the industry as they brought increased resources and greater respectability. And in spite of the banks' massive purchase of much of the U.S. factoring industry, four of the largest practitioners—each with a turnover of more than $1,000M—remained independent in 1973. These four, Walter E. Heller, Meinhard Commercial, United Factors and James Talcott, were, together with the First National Bank of Boston, the biggest factors in the world. In contrast to the increasing absorption of factors by banking groups, Heller possesses its own banking subsidiary.

Factoring in the U.S. has many refinements not possessed by the British counterpart. As in Britain, the American factor provides both 'maturity' and immediate-payment services. However, he is also frequently prepared to lend sums on other assets besides outstanding debts and will make advances of money related to, but not necessarily secured by, the client's inventory. This, they will do because the client's inventory will ultimately be converted into sales, the receivables from which they can then purchase to retire the loan. In fact, this arrangement constitutes an advance of funds against the accounts receivables before their actual creation. This kind of operation can be used to solve the problems of companies with very substantial overdrafts or whose credit strength does not justify an overdraft to buy either stocks or raw materials.

American factors also conduct another type of operation, known as a 'mill agent' or 'drop shipment' arrangement, and similar to that sometimes undertaken, but not widely used, in Britain. It usually involves a client without manufacturing or shipping facilities. Most frequently it entails a new enterprise. When such a company receives a commercial order, it must submit a corresponding order to its own suppliers through the factor. If the factor approves the credit of the ultimate buyer, it signs a guarantee to the client's suppliers. This guarantee is the essence of a 'drop shipment' arrangement.

The guarantee may take the following form:

'We guarantee the payment of the bill arising from the sale of merchandise referred to herein, provided the merchandise is delivered to, and finally accepted by, the consignee referred to herein, and provided there are no merchandise disputes, claims, etc. This guarantee does not cover cancellations of any kind and may be terminated in whole or in part by us at any time prior to shipment of the merchandise.

Kindly note that approved bills due to mills and/or vendors maturing during any one week will be paid on Friday of that week.'

This guarantee then permits the client to buy and sell the merchandise simultaneously, without taking physical possession of it. The procedure can be of great support to sales-orientated clients without a credit base. It enables merchandise to be shipped in their name in order that they might become established in their trade. The client's own purchasing order to his suppliers is accompanied by the factor's guarantee, while the bill to the ultimate customer declares that the merchandise has been sold by the client, but that payment is due to the factor. If the initial supplier is a manufacturer without a distribution network, he will also gain, of course, from the additional orders. The client's own account with the factor will reflect the price difference between his sales and his purchases—his gross profit. The proceeds of the purchased accounts receivable will have been set against the accounts payable, and the client's own credit is not, in this way, involved.

A variation of this arrangement occurs with the issuing of a factor's guarantee for merchandise purchased and added to the the client's inventory. Clearly, when this happens the client is not buying and selling simultaneously. But, here, the factor may have the freshly purchased inventory pledged to him, or he may, in some cases, place reliance on the financial position of the client, of which he will have an intimate knowledge. The inventory-building guarantee allows the client to use his credit balance with the factor (whether already created or to be created out of future sales) to obtain the stocks necessary to conduct his business.

American factors also provide secured inventory loans and other forms of financial accommodation.

The normal duration of an account receivable in the U.S. ranges between ten and 180 days. In a credit-conscious country where all the larger corporations are given credit ratings, its value as a near-liquid asset is not underrated (as it has been for so long in Britain) and for the smaller company, most in need of finance, the early conversion of receivables into cash assumes particular importance in the competitive American commercial climate. A brief examination of the company failure rate quickly demonstrates this point.

In recent time new companies have been formed in the U.S. at the rate of some 400,000 a year, with 25,000 set up in New York alone. But an equally large number cease trading for one reason or another—bankruptcy, liquidation, death, or simply because the rewards were smaller than expected. The actual failure rate has ranged between 9,000 and 16,000 a year and the level of liabilities involved has tended to run at between \$1,000M and \$2,000M. However, the 1969–70 recession in the U.S. resulted in an increase in the number of failures and a sharp jump in the liabilities owed by the defaulting companies. The number of failures rose by some 17 per cent, while the total current liabilities of the failed companies leapt by a hefty 65 per cent, indicating that many of the larger firms were also suffering from the

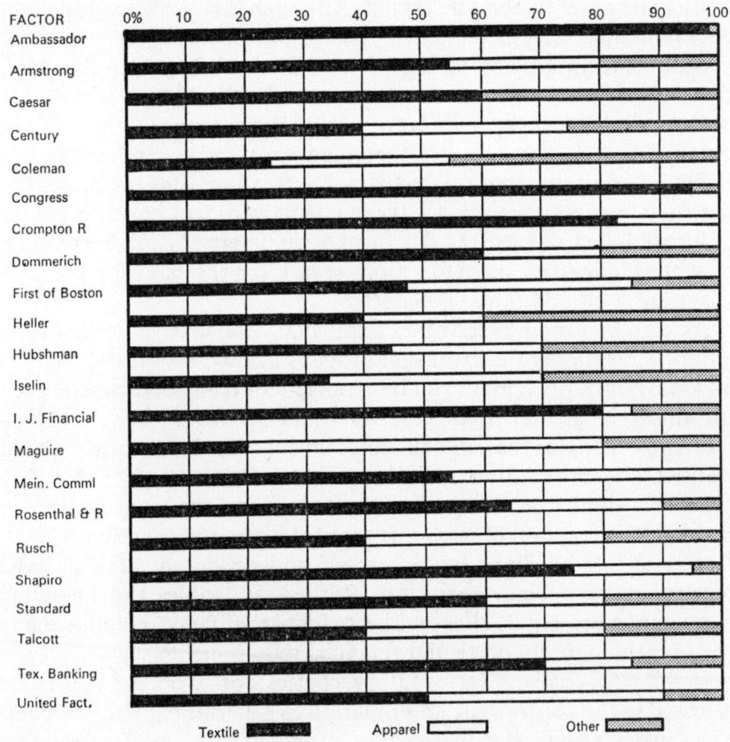

Figure 18. Industry breakdown of U.S. factoring turnover.

harsher economic climate. Most significantly, around 15 per cent of the failures involving manufacturing companies was attributable to liquidity problems caused by difficulties in obtaining payment for deliveries.

It is the small, often newly formed company, with a limited amount of capital and a rising volume of receivables, that has proved the archetypal client of American factors. Although some corporations with annual sales of $50M are factored, the main concentration of clients falls in the $5M to $15M turnover category. In most cases, companies with sales of as little as $500,000 would be acceptable to a factor.

Receivables Financing in the U.S.

In addition to their increasing involvement in factoring, some banks participate in receivables financing. Although this participation dates back to immediately after the war, receivables financing never became a significant proportion of banks' total business loans. In this field, the most active banks are the large ones in the bigger population centres. But generally they have always been wary of this type of operation. It is not a service they tend to stress and relatively few banks have set up separate departments to administer them, confining their business mainly to those clients who can be expected to graduate soon to a more regular form of commercial bank borrowing, or whose loans can be made more secure for the bank by the provision of good additional collateral.

As with factoring, receivables financing has also developed several adjuncts, including the extension of loans against inventory, chattels and real estate. Such loans can be arranged for companies whose need for funds is greater than can be obtained from their accounts receivables. In this case, merchandise inventories, for example, would be used to secure additional working capital in the same way that they are under similar factoring arrangements. Thus, the loans are repaid through the creation of accounts receivables as merchandise is sold. Rarely is this ancillary lending made independently of the basic receivables financing operation. Rather, it enables the financing company to present its client with a 'package' of facilities tailor-made to accommodate its particular financial requirements.

In this way, receivables, inventory, chattel mortgages and real estate are used in the appropriate combination to generate capital. If a company needs a million dollars for a given purpose, and its accounts receivable permit the advance of only $450,000 from the finance company, a further $250,000 might be obtained, under the 'package' concept, against inventory, while chattel mortgages might raise a further $150,000, with the balance covered by a real estate loan.

Rates of commission on receivables financing arrangements usually range between 1/40th and 1/24th of 1 per cent per day, which translated to simple interest rate terms on an annual basis, is 9 to 15 per cent (but this is, of course, dependent on the prevailing level of interest rates generally). This charge is calculated on a daily basis and levied on the sums in use. A typical example of a line of credit granted by a commercial finance company, of say $500,000, might be constructed like this: 80 per cent advance on all accounts receivable not over 90 days old, a supplementary inventory loan not to exceed $200,000 or 50 per cent of the cost of raw materials and 70 per cent of the finished merchandise, and a second mortgage on the borrower's machinery and equipment as additional collateral.

Almost all the commercial financing companies and factoring houses in the U.S. are members of the National Commercial Finance Conference, the national trade association. This was set up in 1945 with just 17 members but today membership has grown to well over a hundred.

Factoring in Europe

European factoring began in Britain, but very quickly spread to West Germany and Sweden. These three countries still have the largest

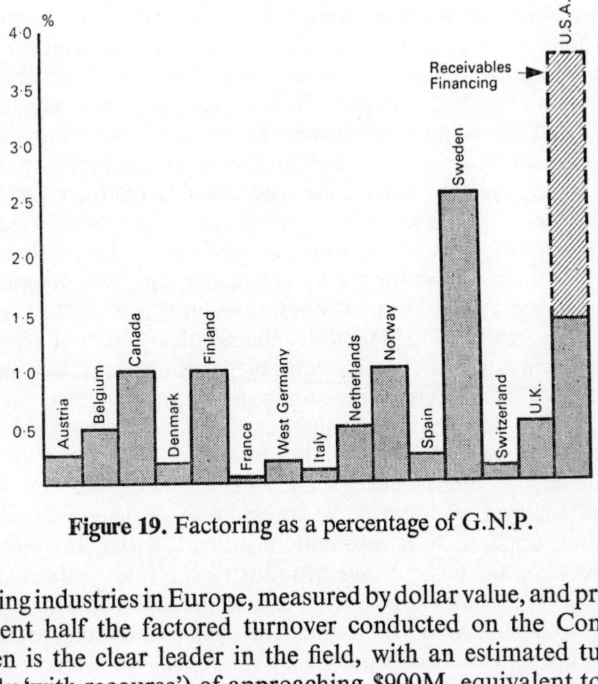

Figure 19. Factoring as a percentage of G.N.P.

factoring industries in Europe, measured by dollar value, and probably represent half the factored turnover conducted on the Continent. Sweden is the clear leader in the field, with an estimated turnover (mainly 'with recourse') of approaching $900M, equivalent to about 2½ per cent of that nation's gross national product. In money terms, Britain probably has the second largest industry and Germany the third largest, amounting, respectively, to about $700M and $500M in 1972, or equivalent to about 0·5 per cent and 0·2 per cent of their gross national products. (In making international comparisons it is more appropriate to measure factoring in G.N.P. terms, rather than by dollar value as this provides a better guide to its importance in the national economy.)

Although in most European countries, factoring is still a much under-developed form of financing, it is growing rapidly in several places, notably Italy and Spain. In 1963 there were only seven or eight factoring companies on the whole continent, by 1971, the figure was estimated to as high as 75 or 80 companies. Germany alone has about 15, Sweden about 10. This compares with about 30 in the United States and 7 in Canada (turnover in Canada is about $1,000M). Elsewhere, Israel, Mexico, Japan, Hong Kong, Singapore, and the Philippines, each have only one active factoring company. In Europe, Greece is one of the few countries without a factoring interest of any sort.

However, there are a number of very distinct differences between the factoring industries on the eastern side of the Atlantic and that in the U.S. Although less mature, factoring in Europe was from the outset backed by banks or other financial institutions and is consequently more closely identified with them. It is viewed essentially as a banking service. In addition, the greater proportion of factoring in Europe tends to be of a 'with recourse' nature, and most companies provide this type of arrangement as well as 'non-recourse.' In contrast, the American old-line factor almost exclusively provides a 'non-recourse' service, the principal division being between this, on the one hand, and receivables financing on the other. The reason for the development in Europe of the hybrid form of operation known as 'with recourse' factoring, is probably explained by the relatively limited experience and availability of credit insurance on the Continent. At the same time because of the prosperous economic conditions of post-war years, losses on trade debts have been light and the business community has underrated the value of such insurance.

A further difference between the factoring industries of the two continents is that while the U.S. houses are still heavily involved in the textile, apparel, footwear and furniture sectors, the European factor serves a far larger range of industries. Notably, these include the service industries, where 'with recourse' arrangements have proved most appropriate. Swiss companies for example, factor the debts of doctors, lawyers and other professional people. Yet another distinctive aspect of the European factor is the greater volume of export-import trade usually handled. This is largely because of the much greater part that such business plays in the economies of the smaller country. As a consequence, international business has a far larger potential. Almost every medium-size European factor sees at least a minor part of its turnover dispatched to foreign markets. Finally, there are often very different attitudes and conventions between the two continents towards credit. In America credit information is a far more developed art. Britain falls some way behind in this respect, but it is still a long way ahead of other European nations. Because of this, and the desire of most manufacturers to preserve their credit ratings, the payment impulse amongst U.S. companies usually begins with receipt of the invoice. In Britain, at least, the impulse frequently starts on receipt of a reminder.

Like their British counterparts, Continental factors have suffered many problems and a good number of frauds in their short history. In Italy, one factoring company sank into serious financial difficulties and had to be rescued by a major bank which was forced to provide substantial amounts of new capital and reconstruct its operations. Both the Heller group and the First National Bank of Boston encountered troubles in their Danish operations.

Again, Sofinter of France suffered a tremendous fraud, which temporarily brought factoring to a halt in that country. This particular factor was formed in 1965 by six large French deposit banks—Crédit Lyonnais, Société Générale, Banque Nationale pour le Commerce et l'Industrie, Comptoir National d'Escompte de Paris (the last two named have subsequently merged) Crédit Commercial and Crédit du Nord.

These six banks decided, in spite of the keen American desire to participate, to establish the factoring company without the involvement of more experienced foreign groups. They also set up a confirming house (a new activity only recently introduced into France). The factor's operation was limited initially to exporting and importing but later extended its business to the domestic French market, believing this more necessary if Sofinter was to keep abreast of its competitors. It grew very rapidly and in one year alone accepted 150 new clients. This explosive growth may have contributed to its downfall. In the event, when Sofinter suffered a serious fraud in 1970, the banks considered their positions and decided to withdraw their backing from the factor, winding up its operations.

Because of several unhelpful legal statutes and the generally rigorous control of financial matters by the French authorities, factoring in that country has been difficult from its beginning in 1964. Backed by the First National Bank of Boston and several large local institutions, Société Francaise de Factoring opened the way for French factoring, negotiating for a considerable time with the Conseil National du Crédit, the main authority concerned, for the necessary authorization to begin business. The Conseil National insisted that any organizations performing factoring in France would have to adopt the compulsory status of a 'financial establishment.' This meant:

(*a*) Membership of the Association Professionnelle d'Etablissements Financiers;

(*b*) Acceptance of the control of the Conseil National du Crédit. As with all financial establishments, factoring companies have to provide twice a year detailed information about their financial situation. In addition, they are not permitted to receive deposits from the public and they must always maintain a fixed ratio between the value of the banking commitments and the amount of their own capital. Inspectors from the Conseil National du Crédit can at any time come and check their financial records.

In spite of these obstacles, by the end of the 1960s there were three principal factoring companies in France, all either subsidiaries of big French banks or foreign networks, or both, and financed either by their bank shareholders or by raising money directly from the French financial market.

Factoring in France, however, has one further major obstacle to overcome. This is the historical and entrenched use of bills of exchange for domestic trade. Because the vast majority of trade debts take this form, there would appear to be rather clear limitations to the growth of factoring within the French home market, although for export-import business there are fewer constraints. Currently, total French factoring turnover is estimated at $50M—$100M.

On the other hand Sweden would seem to be a 'natural' market for factoring. It developed as a response to a particularly severe credit 'squeeze' in the early 1960s, and the ability of factoring houses to receive long-term deposits has contributed to its subsequent growth. At the same time, Swedish industry is very sophisticated in its book-keeping and accounting. For this reason factoring has been viewed as a natural extension of established practices. The general preoccupation with overseas trade was reflected in the early contributions of Swedish factors to the formation of Factors Chain International. Although the other Scandinavian countries also have growing factoring industries, the Swedish houses account for two-thirds of total factored turnover throughout that area of Europe.

The considerable trade between Sweden and Britain has given a special significance to the close factoring links between the two countries. Britain is Sweden's largest market, accounting for about 15 per cent of its exports. Of its imports, some 13 per cent come from Britain. As they possess the two largest and most mature factoring industries in Europe, there is clearly enormous scope for increasing the volume of this bilateral trade conducted on a factored open-account basis.

Moreover, as West Germany is Sweden's second largest market and the largest sources of its imports, and Britain and Germany themselves also loom large in each others foreign trade, the potential for factors to exploit their growing influence in these three countries is quite considerable. This triangular relationship could prove both a valuable nucleus and a powerful springboard for obtaining the ultimate objective of integrated, high-volume factoring operations throughout Europe. The consequent economies of scale that would follow such a development would cause the costs of domestic and international factoring to converge, thereby making the export services no dearer than those provided for business in the home market.

Until comparatively recently, the problems associated with trade credit and non-payment of debts, were virtually unknown in Germany. The German economic 'miracle' and generally growing national affluence had kept corporate financial difficulties at bay. But, more recently, inflation and the various stringent measures adopted by the Federal Government to deal with that phenomenon, has made life more difficult for many enterprises. Company insolvencies were increasing at a rate of some 14 per cent in Germany during 1973. Company failures and the fear of them has had a salutary effect on collective corporate attitudes. This, together with periodic official 'tight money' policies, has contributed to the growth of factoring in that country.

However, even now average payment periods in Germany are only about 45 days, compared with the rather longer time taken by customers to settle their debts in Britain and elsewhere. In addition, there is one unique legal problem facing German factors which could speed payments in a rather unusual way. The law provides a manufacturer with certain titles to goods sold, and the receivables arising from subsequent re-sales (the principle of 'extended property') through to the ultimate buyer in the manufactoring chain. Thus, if a factor's client does not pay his own suppliers, then that supplier may have recourse both to the client's customers and to the factor. As a consequence, the factor will be keen not only to arrange speedy collection of debts owed to the client, but also to affirm that the client's own outstanding bills are paid.

Most of the 14 factors in Germany are bank owned because non-bank factoring houses labour under particular disadvantages over the charging of interest. German factoring is also peculiarly regional. Although in the northern part of the country it is a well established industry, in the south it is still little known or understood. Even in the north, there are some factors who conduct no domestic business, but operate exclusively in the international arena, reflecting the priorities and preoccupations of German manufacturing industry as a whole.

After Germany, Britain and Sweden, the countries with the next largest factoring industries (in dollar value terms) are the Netherlands, with roughly $250M turnover, Belgium, with perhaps, $200M,

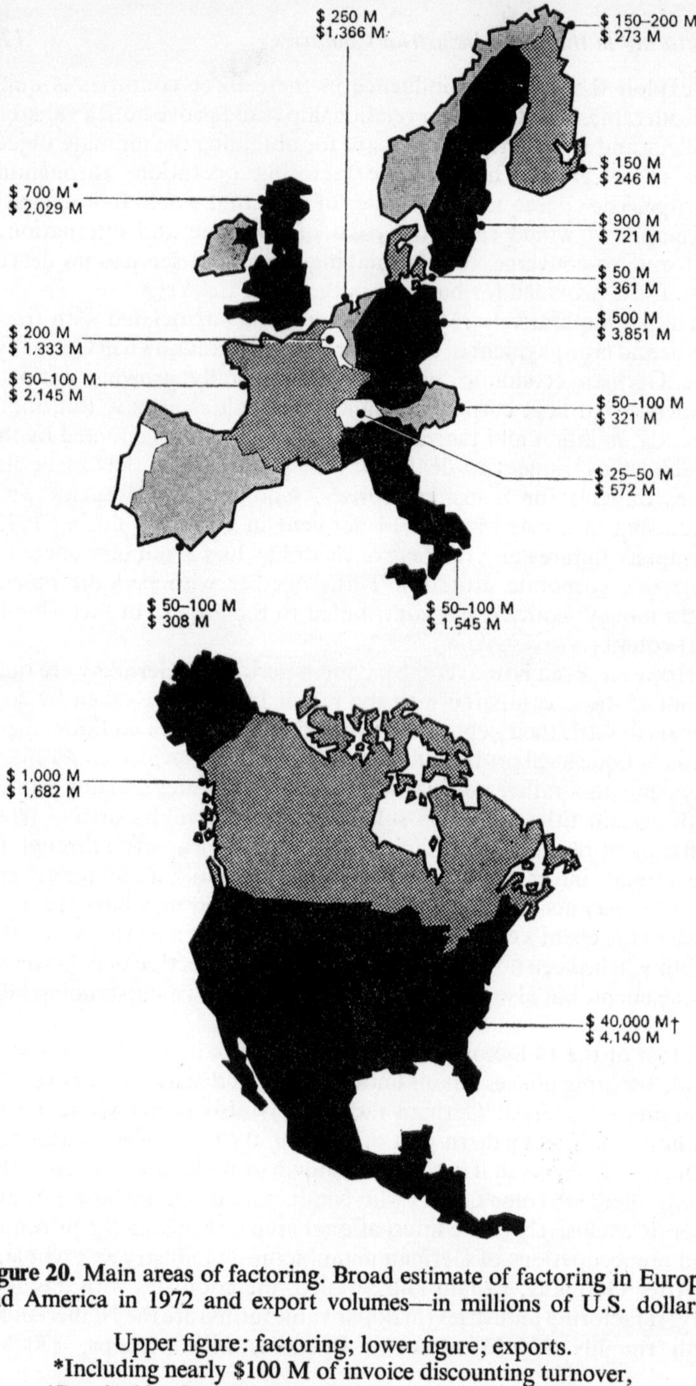

Figure 20. Main areas of factoring. Broad estimate of factoring in Europe and America in 1972 and export volumes—in millions of U.S. dollars.

Upper figure: factoring; lower figure; exports.
*Including nearly $100 M of invoice discounting turnover,
†Receivables financing accounts for 60 per cent of this total.

Norway, with between $150M and $200M, and Finland, with about $150M. As a percentage of these countries' gross national products, their factoring turnover represents very roughly ½ per cent each for the two Benelux countries and 1 per cent each for the two Scandinavian countries. Belgium is notable for the high volume of its overseas factored turnover (50 per cent of the total), which is not surprising, perhaps, for a country whose exports account for some 40 per cent of its gross domestic product.

In the lower league division are Italy and France with a factoring industry of between $100M and $150M; Austria and Spain with about $50M; and Switzerland with something between $25M and $50M. However, in most countries of Western Europe these volumes are growing. Amongst the latter group the Latin countries—Spain and Italy—appear to offer particularly favourable conditions for the rapid expansion of factoring. This is in spite of, or perhaps because of, the generally unpropitious financial climate in Italy in recent years. Wide sectors of Italian industry failed to make a profit in 1971–72 and, while making factoring more hazardous for its practitioners, this must certainly increase its attractiveness to potential users. At the same time the exports of Italy include a considerable proportion of low-technology, mass-consumer goods, which are ideal for factoring.

The steady industrialization and low labour costs of Spain means that its exports will increasingly be of a similar kind. Moreover, it has shown a keen interest in adopting and emulating the financial and management techniques of its more industrially advanced neighbours. The Spanish economy began to expand rapidly towards the close of 1971 and in 1972 its gross national product rose, in real terms, by 7½ per cent—one of the highest growth rates among European countries. Its imports have also expanded sharply. During the five years to 1972 its imports from Britain rose by no less than 84 per cent, from £92·5M in 1967 to £170·6M in 1972. Notwithstanding Spain's comparatively unsophisticated financial infrastructure, it already has five factoring houses operating within its borders.

Outside America and Europe, South Africa has one of the most rapidly developing factoring industries, with three principal companies accounting for a turnover of about $100M to $150M

9 Case Studies

There are numerous companies on the British factors' files which have profited richly from their services. Amongst two of the best known companies to whose ultimate success the factoring technique contributed are Buxted Chicken and Dexion. In spite of the confidentiality of the factor-client relationship, the circumstances of these arrangements have become public knowledge, perhaps because of the glamour that has at some time in the past attached to their names. But Buxted Chicken is interesting for another reason. An arrangement was reached between it and International Factors which was probably unique and reveals the inherent flexibility that factoring can achieve.

Buxted was factored for about six years, from 1964 to the beginning of 1970, when after a series of takeovers (throughout which it continued to be factored) it was finally absorbed by Imperial Tobacco, a company that had more than sufficient cash for the requirements of its new subsidiary. Set up as Poultry Packers (Sussex) Ltd. in 1955, Buxted became a public company around 1960. In its early days at least, it was regarded as one of the 'high flyers' of the Stock Exchange lists. Its business was the processing and marketing of young broiler chickens ready for cooking. It also sold broiler equipment and provided general advisory, costing and other technical services in connection with chicken production. Initially, it sold to one large retailer, but the range of its customers steadily widened. Yet, by 1964, the company was suffering many difficulties. The price of its shares had dropped sharply and it had become prey to takeover bids, finally being bought by a larger group called Allied Farm Foods. The factoring arrangement which dates from about this time was uninterrupted by this event.

A rationalization of the broiler industry was taking place and many of the small firms involved were going out of business. Moreover, a good number of Buxted's customers presented high-risk situations. For example, one customer with capital of just £7,000 was buying £20,000 worth of Buxted produce a week. As a result, Buxted was utilizing £1M of advances from International Factors at any one time. As this was becoming an alarming state of affairs, it was necessary to arrive at some fresh, mutually acceptable arrangement to safeguard the interests of both Buxted and the factor.

A formula was devised whereby a contingency fund could be built up in case of an emergency, but which allowed reimbursement if, in the event, the money was not needed. This scheme required Buxted to pay an extra 0·4 per cent of its turnover to International Factors to cover possible bad debts, but provided for a 90 per cent rebate where debt losses were not incurred. With the assistance of this arrangement, enabling the continued support of the factor, Buxted staged a considerable recovery, emerged from the industry rationalization as one of the larger poultry groups and returned to the ranks of those companies with profits to distribute. Allied Farm Foods, the Buxted parent, was later taken over by Associated British Foods in the Autumn of 1968 and the latter-named group was itself absorbed by Imperial Tobacco some little time later. In passing, it may be of some interest to note that the value of Allied Farm Foods' debtors was still rising sharply, following the termination of the factoring agreement, increasing in the twelve months to October 31, 1971 from £5·7M to £8M (the company's accounts continued to be prepared separately after the takeovers). This could have presented considerable problems to a company lacking the confident backing of Imperial Tobacco.

During the period that Buxted was factored, its sales rose from £10M to £17M and its debt losses were sharply reduced. Such losses, which frequently ran at £20,000 a year, declined to a mere £200 in one twelve-month period. If this proved one of its best years, it was nonetheless true that in other years too, the level of losses was kept within tolerable bounds, given the high-risk nature of the business and the adverse trading conditions then prevailing. Factoring for Buxted Chicken provided not so much a 'launching pad' for success—for which there are many other examples—but, more importantly in this case, demonstrated its nursing and convalescent qualities.

Dexion Ltd, like Buxted Chicken, also entered into a factoring agreement around 1964. The history of Dexion actually dates back to 1937, but it was not until after the war that it began to pioneer the steel slotted angle sections for which it has become widely known. These slotted angle sections form versatile and universal construction systems, a kind of do-it-yourself material for light structures in industry and commerce, particularly in the fields of industrial storage. Marketing its products in over 100 countries, the parent group, Dexion-Comino International, is the world's largest manufacturer of slotted angle. Immediately after the earthquake disaster at Skopje, Yugoslavia in 1963, the company provided materials for, and supervized, the erection of two complete new villages, one of which was called Dexiongrad.

Since 1968, the company's shares have been quoted on the Stock Exchange. It is one of the few companies that has had to declare in its prospectus that 'most of the trade debts of the company relating to sales in the United Kingdom are sold to a factor without recourse to the Company on terms whereby the purchased price of each debt is payable by the factor 69 days after the conclusion of its sale'. Debtors of Dexion Ltd, at October 31, 1967 included £770,000 owed until 'due date' by the factor, after deducting £231,000 advanced by the factor to the company.

Like so many companies that have been factored, the precise benefit of the arrangement is difficult to quantify because it is impossible to say how it would have fared otherwise. It can only be judged on the company's track record. In fact Dexion Ltd has seen its sales doubled in recent years to £10M, although in line with other parts or the group it suffered a major profits setback in 1971. Turnover of the whole Dexion-Comino group has risen even faster from £8·9M in 1964 to £10·6M in 1967 and £30M in 1971, when the U.K. accounted for some 30 per cent of group sales, against 50 per cent in 1967. But the sharper rise in international sales is hardly surprising since it is marketing in 100 countries.

But, if Buxted Chicken and Dexion can be counted as relative successes for factoring, there have also been the occasional failures. One publicised arrangement which proved less than satisfactory was with the Mary Quant Ginger Group in 1968. It was initiated as an experiment and failed largely because the customers were boutiques where invoice values were small and difficult to collect. As a consequence, the efforts involved were not commensurate with a realistic factoring charge. But other businesses of a not dissimilar kind have proved more successful, notably that of Jeff Banks, husband of pop singer Sandie Shaw, and boutique owner and maker of fashion clothes for outlets in London's West End and abroad.

Some More Successes of Factoring

Perhaps, the case that sums up most dramatically what factoring can achieve is that of a specialist stockists called Manor Building & Plumbing Supplies Ltd, of Epsom. This firm supplies copper tubes and fittings for domestic central heating, industrial heating and plumbing for condensation systems, for building site erection. The range of items it is obliged to carry is large, running to several thousands of types and sizes. The manufacturers of these fittings such as Yorkshire Imperial Metals and the Glynwed and Delta groups do not have the distributing capacity needed to service the large number of constructors involved. As a result, the sub-contractors and even the contractors, such as Wimpey and Watts find it convenient to send purchasing orders for fittings—the precise variety required often dictated by consulting engineers' specifications—to stockists who deliver straight to the site at short notice.

Manor Building and Plumbing was started around 1962–63 by Frank Hayward and Frederick Grey with £100 capital in a small lock-up shop. But, as the venture grew, so increasingly they found they needed more cash to finance expansion. Many of the company's 300 customers took months to pay for the delivered goods, particularly if they themselves were committed to an 18-month or two-year job, and were only receiving progress payments. Many customers took three or four months to pay, while a fair proportion took even five or six months.

By around the turn of 1971, anything up to £50,000 might have been outstanding to the partners of Manor Building and Plumbing at any one time. This was on a monthly turnover of £30,000 to £40,000 (perhaps £450,000 a year) and a capital base of only £12,000. Their bank, Lloyds, felt it could extend only an overdraft of £3,000 because the Manor warehouse was only rented and there was no collateral which the partners could use to secure a bigger loan. All that they owned was the stock, which tended to be turned over at least once a month on average (many items turning over even more quickly). The convention in the trade is for payment to be made at the end of the month following the month in which delivery is made. Where settlement is made on the due date, a 2½ per cent discount is usually given.

So desperate were the partners that they themselves were sacrificing their own discount from their suppliers to gain an extra month in which to pay for their stock, a particularly expensive practice on such a rapid turnover. Lloyds Bank referred them to its group associate, International Factors. The partners of Manor Building were considered by International Factors and approved. Even by factoring standards the improvement that followed in the financial position of the stockist was dramatic.

Immediately, 70 per cent of the outstanding debt figure was released, enabling the Manor partners to settle their own bills. They quickly saved £15,000 simply by paying their bills on the standard settlement basis and taking the 2½ per cent discount. They were even able to enjoy discounts of 3¾ per cent which were occasionally offered to them for debts settled in cash within seven days. During the first year of the factoring agreement turnover expanded 80 per cent. Although the pace of growth slowed a little in the following months, it was still considerable, with turnover running at between £140,000 and £160,000 a month by the end of 1972. Profits rose more than proportionately, from £30,000 gross in the 1970–71 financial year (before the factoring agreement) to some £150,000 gross in 1972–73.

Additionally, there were particular advantages in having the factor conduct the sales ledger and accounts operation, because of the limitations on office space at the Manor warehouse. The factor's pressure on the debtors brought down the average length of debt settlement periods. Although some initial resentment was generated by the use of a factor in collection work, this was short-lived and no customers were actually lost. The very occasional refusal of the factor to accept a new Manor customer proved no obstacle as the partners took the view that such a refusal was in their own interest. Their rapid growth led to possibilities of opening new depots to extend the firm's geographical coverage and—in the more distant future—the chances of going public. The partners' bank declared a willingness to lend them £100,000 for expansion.

P. R. Roast & Company was a small family concern which also experienced considerable difficulty in obtaining sufficient finance for the business from its bank. Formed in 1964, Roast is engaged in the importing and marketing of china, pottery and glassware. The company is run by its founder, Mr P. R. Roast and his two sons. They started with a limited amount of capital and almost immediately found that if they were able to achieve the kind of turnover which was available and necessary, they needed financial assistance. Various clearing banks and merchant banks were approached, but as the company had no strong collateral to offer, they found that they were too small commercially, to provoke any interest in these institutions. As the company's turnover was less than £100,000 per annum, even a number of factors felt unable to help the Roast family.

However, if a company possesses a clear growth potential, the factoring industry is usually flexible enough to accommodate even smaller than average clients. In this case, an approach was made to Alex Lawrie Factors, which has been especially inclined to accept the smaller firm. In July 1968, a factoring agreement was signed. This had an immediate beneficial effect on the particular problem retarding the company's expansion—that of a slow cashflow.

Before being factored Roast had found that, even if the company sold every item that it purchased abroad on the very day that the goods were landed in Britain, some two or three months would still pass before the money would flow in for further use. In contrast with this situation, the factoring agreement provided for a very large proportion of the sale price to be made available on the day the goods were delivered to Roast's customers. It could then re-invest the funds at once in further imports.

There was also an unexpected beneficial side effect of the agreement. When the import restrictions were imposed by the Government shortly after the Roast family became involved in factoring the banks were not generally permitted to finance importers. However, the same restrictions did not apply to the factoring houses—as they did not make loans but purchased the book debts. Initially, P. R. Roast maintained its own sales ledger after the factoring operation began, but it built up sufficient faith in the factor's computerized accounting systems to put aside its own ledgers subsequently and allow Alex Lawrie total control of this side of the administration.

The company's annual sales exceeded £200,000 in 1971, or £300,000 if other, wider activities are included. This compares with a turnover of a mere £19,000 per annum when the factoring agreement was signed. The original capital of £100, has been increased to over £10,000 paid up. Its trading position has been given a solid basis and its future expansion assured.

Yet, the cash problems caused by Roast's imports were no more acute than many faced by exporters. For one Northern England company selling to France, the liquidity difficulties confronted seriously undermined its financial position. It specialized in working scale-models of mechanical and electrical equipment, and scientific apparatus (simulation tanks, electric motors, refrigeration systems and the like). Much of the company's output was sold abroad to universities and educational establishments, particularly in France.

However, the French authorities were never entirely reconciled to having to purchase this equipment from abroad. Although there was never any doubt that payment for all such French imports would eventually be forthcoming, officialdom was extremely dilatory in actually making the settlement, with numerous rubber stamps necessary and many a bureaucrat's signature required. It was not uncommon for debts to be outstanding for nine months. This was clearly intolerable for a company needing cash to pay the wages of skilled craftsmen, the rates and rent on the work premises, suppliers of materials, transport costs and general overheads.

Comparatively large sums were involved. On an annual turnover of £400,000, anything between a half and two-thirds of sales might be unpaid at any one time (including some non-French debts). Bank finance was available, but a good deal less of it than was required. City institutions were unenthusiastic about the proposition and factors were themselves somewhat deterred by the length of the credit periods involved. In spite of full order books, the possibility of disbanding the design teams and closing the laboratories was in prospect.

However, a trial experiment with a factor was arranged in 1969, as despite the lengthly settlement period on French sales, the risk of default was almost negligible. The arrangement was fully justified. The ready availability of funds helped keep the company in business, while the factor's counterpart in France was able, through its knowledge of the official channels and diplomatic prodding, to bring about a 20 per cent reduction in the settlement procedures. The general improvement in the company's liquidity allowed it to meet the orders received from educational establishments in other parts of the world, which were in danger of being sacrificed because the French commitment represented a longer-standing contract. The factoring arrangement thus paved the way to a steady 20 per cent annual rise in profits over the following three years.

The strength of factoring lies in its ability to accommodate a wide variety of situations. Although most clients have basically common requirements, these frequently differ in the particular. The diverse fields of cleaning materials, advertising and electronics, each provides an example of a specific, if not wholly untypical, situation that confronts factors. The first appertains to an old, established company facing difficulties breaking into a fresh market; the second, to a company making a slow recuperation after an unfortunate incident; and the third, to a new company constrained by lack of capital.

For 80 years R. P. Adam Ltd had been manufacturing a range of cleaning and maintenance products, selling them mainly through retail outlets. But, in 1968, the company decided to turn its attention to the industrial market. For its pains, it recorded a loss that year of £9,500 on a turnover of £20,000. In spite of the unencouraging balance sheet, and although R. P. Adam's sales were considerably less than usually necessary to qualify for a factoring arrangement, the evident growth potential in this field proved sufficiently attractive for such an arrangement to be composed. The funds then released helped sales to rise sharply, by 115 per cent in 1969 and a further 90 per cent in 1970. But profits eluded the company. There was, too, a major disappointment to come when at the last minute, a promised contract from the local county council failed to materialize.

Worst still, with additional cash desperately needed, Adam's bankers, the Bank of Scotland, felt unable to help the company in its predicament. Fortunately, the factor was able to arrange short-term finance through another member of its group. With the aid of this money and the factoring advances, R. P. Adam managed, in 1971, to make its first profit for three years, albeit a small one. Armed with its more cheerful accounts, the Adam's financial director retraced his footsteps to the head office of the Bank of Scotland in the hope of a more sympathetic response to his request for a loan. However, the bank's offer of £5,000 secured on gross free assets of £86,000 brought the meeting to an abrupt end.

As a consequence, the decision was taken to change bankers. In 1972, with a healthy cashflow from factoring, more progressive bankers, and a growing number of customers, R. P. Adams made a profit of more than £32,500 on a turnover of £260,000. This turnover was some 1,200 per cent greater than achieved in 1968—after eight decades of trading! Yet, but for the factor, there is a good chance that the attempt by R. P. Adams to extend its operations into new fields might have precipitated the company's demise.

The future of the company in the second example was also seriously threatened at the time it first entered into a factoring agreement in 1965. It had carried on business as an advertising agency and had been moderately successful. Turnover had risen gradually and amounted to about £200,000. However, its problems were not the result of any trading setback, but were inflicted on the company by one of its directors. This director had pledged the agency's assets to guarantee another company with which he was connected. When this second company ran into difficulties, it came perilously close to dragging down the advertising agency in its wake. At best, the agency was left in a shaky financial position, requiring considerable finance if it was to continue trading and ultimately become profitable again. The factor had the delicate job of reconstituting the company and nursing it back to health. The operation was an unmitigated success. The agency's turnover began to expand rapidly and within four or five years had grown to over £2M per annum.

The third example concerns a dynamic young electronics company which had started with £100 but whose expansion was being retarded by lack of capital. This constraint is a recurring theme encountered by factors and is amply illustrated by this company. It was based in the Midlands and run by two brothers, Dick and Harry. Like so many such companies, it was under-capitalized and in 1967, the problems came to a head. On a turnover of £103,000 the brothers were owed some £22,000 by trade debtors. Dick was a good salesman and Harry a good designer. They were selling to large and small electronics firms but were finding it progressively more difficult to collect their debts. The larger their company grew, the more important the unsettled debts became in the overall balance sheet position. Time and energy were spent on the telephone chasing customers for payment or calling in person on the chief cashier of the debtor. This was time and energy desperately needed in designing and selling the company's products.

The brothers' introduction to a factor and his acceptance of them as clients brought this state of affairs to an early end. The cash provided by the factor was channelled back into research and development. Discounts which the brothers had been forced to offer their customers as an inducement for early debt settlement, were eliminated. Indeed, with more funds available, they soon found that they could pay their own creditors faster and themselves gain quick-payment discounts from their suppliers. But most importantly, the extra investment in research and development began to prove fruitful, producing valuable new additions to their product range. After ten months of factoring, the company's turnover had increased from an annual £103,000 to £161,000 giving profits of £7,900. After two years it had risen to £225,000 a year and profits had climbed to £17,000. The third year saw turnover much higher again, at £300,000 and profits of £25,000.

If these three cases demonstrate the benefits of factoring when coping with some particular situations, its general application as a weapon for countering cyclical downswings may be of equal value in those industries prone to such periodic reductions in demand and output. It is not only at times of economic growth, when markets are expanding, that factoring can be exploited. Some industries, like machine tool manufacture, suffer inordinately during times of economic recession, and the worst effects could at least be partially mitigated by planned counter-cyclical measures.

Athena Semi-conductors Marketing Company of Egham, Surrey illustrates this point. Set up in 1968, Athena's growth has been steady rather than spectacular. A desire to expand without borrowing large sums of money led the company into an arrangement with H. & H. Factors just a year after the company was formed. Its business is distributing, through agency agreements, electronic components manufactured in the U.S., Italy and Britain. Frequently, the company's technical sales engineers will be involved with, say a prototype computer, at the design stage, to facilitate the early marketing of the components. However, because of the nature of its business and the large number of customers—nearly 1,000—Athena has a large number of low value invoices which create considerable paperwork for the factor and result in a factoring fee towards the top end of the scale, at around 2 per cent.

This proved no deterrent to Athena which, together with the factor quickly began devising schemes for lumping together several smaller invoices to the same customer before they were dispatched to the factor, in the hope of cutting his workload and lowering the fee. But, even before this cost-cutting exercise, the factoring arrangement was displaying its worth. The market in which Athena operated had become increasingly depressed. In addition, the price of a semiconductor fell from £12 to £1. The total value of the British market for semi-conductors, which was roughly £63M in 1969, grew to £72M in 1970, but fell sharply to only £60M in 1971, before recovering markedly in 1972, to around £80M.

Yet, in contrast to this sluggish performance for the market as a whole, Athena's turnover more than doubled. In the 21 months to May 31, 1970, it logged sales of £287,000. In the following 12 months, the figure climbed to £370,000, rising to £453,000 in 1971–72, and well in excess of £500,000 in 1972–73. A turnover of more than £1M was confidently predicted within the succeeding two or three years. Although a more favourable climate within the industry might have produced a very much faster growth in Athena's turnover, perhaps leading to the achievement of £1M by 1972–73, the company estimates that but for factoring it would have been at least £100,000 less than actually accomplished. In addition, the company estimates that the factoring arrangement saved it £5,000 a year in direct salary costs, £1,000 annually on bad debts and £500 on telephone, stationery and postal charges. Moreover, there was a saving in office space, a reduction of 15 days in credit taken by customers, a gain from bulk buying (made possible by the improved cashflow), and a lessening of the burden borne by management. In this case, the final net cost would probably be less than the equivalent bank overdraft interest, despite the above-average factoring fee made necessary by the company's low average invoice value.

Similar market conditions to that faced by Athena, also confronted a Coventry company of precision engineers. This enterprise was started with a capital of £500 in the early 1960s. In its early years, it grew steadily, but in the rather bleak conditions of 1969–70, demand contracted and debts piled up. Turnover of the company which had reached a peak of £250,000 began to decline. In the prevailing climate there appeared to be little that it could do, but await an improvement in the general situation, hoping that the economic 'stop' would be followed by 'go', as it had been for much of the post-war years. Less passively, however, the company chose to factor, in an attempt to improve its debtor position and increase its cash resources during this rather difficult period.

The results of this action, perhaps proved more dramatic than expected. A sharp injection of funds from the factor enabled the company to follow a rather aggressive policy within its industry, and it took over two other engineering firms, sharply increasing its total order books. At the same time, rationalization within the enlarged company helped to prune costs, while economies of scale and longer production 'runs' also contributed to a rise in profits. Of no little importance, too, was the marked drop in the company's debt turn, which was reduced by 12 days on average. As one of the companies taken over had a very bad debt position, with many thousands of pounds outstanding, the debtor position in this area was even more dramatically improved. Moreover, the much greater volume of funds now made available by the factor, inflated the enlarged company's liquidity position still more markedly. By the time that the national economy began to move out of the recession, around the second half of 1972, the turnover of the engineering company was running at £600,000 to £700,000 annually. As a footnote to this particular case study, it is of incidental interest that the company became so flush with funds it decided to discontinue its factoring arrangement, believing, not necessarily correctly, that there was little more that the factor could contribute to the success of the business. Thus, the factor had accomplished so much that it had made itself redundant.

But, if economic recession brings problems, economic growth does also, as evidenced by a final brief success story from the factors' files. West Country Gauge had since before the last war been engaged in the manufacture of gauges and tools. Its growth was only gradual until the middle 1960s when a more thrusting management and more competitive pricing policies produced a sharp expansion of business. With order books full and no spare production capacity, it became necessary to invest in new buildings and machinery. But, the greater output and the concentration on winning orders resulted in a considerable deterioration in the debtor position. Customers were taking several weeks longer to pay and large sums were owed to the company.

Although turnover had been increased in two years from £300,000 to over £500,000, so much capital was tied up in the debtors that West Country Gauge had insufficient funds to make the necessary investments. The company had little wish to make a public issue of shares and was not entirely happy with the size of the loan offered by its bankers. A meeting was arranged between the company's executives and representatives of a factor which culminated in an agreement being signed. Within weeks of this agreement, the factor was able to make a considerable dent in the level of outstanding debts. The immediate release of funds allowed West Country Gauge to purchase additional work space and order new machinery. It was able to meet its customers' orders and, additionally, to accept fresh commitments. Turnover continued the rapid growth set in train two-and-a-half years earlier, with a commensurate expansion in profits.

Some Failures of Factoring

Of course factoring has had its failures as well as its successes. These have occurred for numerous reasons. For some clients it may be simply that the management, while adequate for a small company, is not strong enough to administer a fast growing enterprise. Again, it may transpire that a client which appeared to have considerable growth potential later fails to live up to its early promise. In such circumstances the factoring commission could prove to be burdensome. Equally, the client might lack the competence to control the large amounts of money made available through factoring. Some clients have used these funds for speculative rather than more directly productive purposes. In some cases, clients have become too ambitious, precipitating their own downfall. Yet, other clients have been unintentionally induced through factoring to overtrade. In some instances factoring has simply proved inappropriate to the particular line of business conducted by the client. This most frequently happened in the early days of factoring in Britain.

There is also the client who, because of the apparently easy money to be obtained from the factor, is tempted into fraudulent practice, or out of over optimism slips into the habit of sending invoices to the factor prematurely. In neither case does this necessarily represent wilful and premeditated dishonesty. It is rather that seemingly easy money can always present a temptation. The factor must be on guard against all of these possibilities. It is for these reasons, that the factor is keen to discover to what purposes the additional money will be put, and why he is keen to see that the cash is quickly put to work in the business. For these reasons again, he will wish to monitor the results. He will require monthly statements in some cases, not because he necessarily wishes such regular details of business progress, but because it is essential that the client himself is aware at any given moment how his money is employed and whether a profit is being made.

An example of a client who, because of a combination of inflated ambition and inadequate management systems, was brought to an abrupt end, is drawn from the air ventilation industry. The company in question was a London-based manufacturer of air treatment, fuel extraction and ventilation equipment. Amongst its products was a device for enabling air to enter houses located near airports while at the same time baffling the noise. Another product was a warm air curtain which directed warm air downwards to keep premises at reasonable temperatures when doors were left open.

Although, in 1965, this company's turnover was only £50,000—rather less than some factors would consider—it was in a challenging growth market and offered products with a very good potential. Its growth indeed proved as dramatic as expected, following the signing of the factoring agreement. But, this success and the availability of the factor's cash, led to an untempered policy of taking over other companies, some even larger than itself. Its turnover climbed sharply to £1M, but with effectively only one man at the helm, its management systems could not cope with such rapid growth.

It became clear that the company's information about its trading position was far from adequate. The factor persuaded its client to employ an independent auditor to check the books. This showed that the company had unknowingly been making substantial losses but also indicated that these were being reduced and that it was again close to a position of profitability. However, the company's weaknesses were impossible to correct. The necessary information, which should have given advance warning of a fresh deterioration were inherently inadequate. When the worst was later revealed it was too late to conduct the kind of measures needed successfully to cut overheads or reduce production. After four years of factoring the company became insolvent. Its decline was almost certainly faster than it would have been without the money made available by the factoring agreement.

Another factoring agreement which failed to live up to expectations, this time less disastrously, concerned a client selling printing machinery. This particular agreement in fact lasted less than a year. Its termination was brought about by a shift in the mix of business conducted by the client. Initially, this printing machinery company sold 20 per cent of its output on hire purchase, with the remainder sold on normal trade credit terms. For this 80 per cent, the client required the regular services of the factor, who made advance payments and collected the debts in the usual way.

However, during the course of the ensuing months, the client increasingly sold on hire purchase until this line of business accounted for 80 per cent of output. As the hire purchase companies took control of the customer's debt repayments and paid the printing machinery manufacturer the full value of the sale, the factoring agreement became rapidly redundant and the factor's commission increasingly onerous. Although the factor offered to charge the manufacturer a lower rate of commission, this was not entirely to his satisfaction and the agreement was brought to an end.

Another episode where a client was lost to a factor because extraneous events occurred in the international field. This concerned a company soliciting and hiring out British technical staff to West German firms. In this case problems arose because this activity attracted German value added tax. The tax had to be collected and transferred to the local authorities before payments could be remitted, and this caused considerable difficulties and delays. As the factor involved had no direct factoring connections in Germany, the client was forced to obtain the services of a local agent to do much of the work. As a result the client decided to cancel his agreement with the British factor and enter a new one with a German factor.

Fraud is an all too common reason for a factoring arrangement turning sour. One example is sufficient to demonstrate the form such abuse might take and the conditions under which it might briefly prevail. In 1965 a factoring arrangement was established with a company effectively controlled by an Austrian-born businessman. He specialized in buying scrapped steel tubes and re-selling them. Essentially, these steel tubes were retrieved from scrapped paper-making machinery and sold to paper makers needing them for replacement in still active machinery.

As this businessman was highly recommended by one of the major joint stock banks, the factor had few qualms in accepting him as a client. Moreover, he appeared prosperous, lived in some luxury and surrounded himself with valuable artistic possessions. But difficulties arose almost from the outset. The client requested larger sums than he was legitimately entitled to claim on the strength of the invoices alone. The factor was persuaded to 'bend' his rules and allowed the client to collect some of his own trade debts. It quickly became clear that this was an unsatisfactory arrangement; the debts were not being collected and were in some cases three months overdue. New invoices directed through the factor were not even sufficient to match previous invoices on which money had been advanced. Yet, still the client demanded more cash for his business.

The wrangle between the parties became acrimonious, with the client insisting that the agreement entitled him to further cash against the new invoices. For the factor, the situation was now intolerable and the agreement was cancelled. Although the client had furnished the factor with a personal gurantee, when the latter attempted to activate it, the house of the Austrian-born businessman was found to have been completely emptied of valuables and the residence sold to his sister. The factor was forced to write off £54,000—a sum greater than its entire capital at that time. Long court cases were consequently set in train. To the factor's dismay, it was only subsequently discovered that this ex-client had previously been bankrupted, and that during the life of the agreement he had claimed money on goods which had not been shipped, issued credit notes unknown to the factor, caused debts to be collected twice and had simultaneously been factored by two other factors.

Two further case studies will serve, as nearly as is possible in a field so rich with variety, to complete a broad picture of the potential problems that might thwart the fruition of a factoring arrangement. The first centres on an old-established plumbing contractor. Only rarely will a factor today approve a prospective client in a trade involving progress payments, for the obvious reason that debtors can not be obliged to pay for uncompleted work. But there have been exceptions in the past which clearly demonstrate the unsuitability of such trades to a factoring arrangement.

The plumbing contractor had grown unspectacularly over the years, and had a turnover of around £100,000 when approved for factoring. In spite of its unexceptional past performance, it had a commendable reputation in its field. Although its sales were declining and losses were being suffered, there was some confidence that careful nursing by a factor could reverse this trend. However, the client's problems proved to lie more directly than suspected in the poor quality of its management. Moreover, it operated in an industry with special problems with which the factor was unequipped to deal. Within a year, the plumbing contractor went out of business. It had been advanced sizeable sums but much of its work remained to be completed and the factor was unable to collect money on work unfinished. Fortunately, another contractor was found to complete the work for which payments were ultimately made. But losses were avoided more by luck than by judgement.

The final example of an unsuccessful factoring arrangement is drawn from the furniture trade and concerns a Yorkshire-based manufacturer. This company was less than five years old when it began factoring, and already it had a turnover of £350,000. It made brightly coloured fashion furniture from plastics and fibreglass, and other modern materials, selling through a large number of high street shops. Although factoring produced a 100 per cent jump in turnover within two years, this simply stimulated fresh ambitions within the company. It rapidly increased output and quickly raised the pace of its expansion to an unsustainable level. In spite of the increased cashflow, it began producing and selling at a rate that could not be supported on the limited capital base of the company. Money was borrowed from several independent sources. New premises were rented and the workforce increased at an alarming rate.

Although the factor became increasingly worried that the furniture maker would be seriously threatened by the first major setback that the company encountered, it was chary of cancelling the arrangement for fear of precipitating just such a crisis. When the pace of the client's momentum faltered and its suppliers and workforce could not be paid by further borrowing, the edifice crumbled. Unmistakably, it was the early success generated by the factor which awakened the insatiable appetite for growth that could not be controlled. Because of this kind of situation, factors have become acutely conscious of the responsibilities they have to the client to ensure that the sums advanced are employed wisely and that his own best interests are protected.

Factoring and the Tufters

In addition to assisting individual companies, factoring can be of benefit on a much broader plane, contributing substantially to the development of whole industries, In the U.S., during the 19th century, it played a crucial role in the growth of the indigenous textile industry. More recently, it was partly responsible for the emergence of the American tufted carpet industry. Before the Second World War, almost all of the carpeting manufactured in the U.S., and in fact in the world, was loomed. This was an expensive process and many consumers could not afford to carpet their homes extensively.

Much of the carpeting sold in the U.S. was actually imported from Belgium, where it was woven by well-established companies. In the domestic American industry, a large proportion was catered for by several old-line factors. But, meanwhile, in Georgia, bedspreads were being manufactured by a process known as 'tufting'. This process constituted the sewing of individual tufts of fibre onto sheets of material, generally cotton. It involved the use of single needle sewing machines which produced one row of tufts at a time.

Although this was an interesting development, it was only of limited significance until other innovators in America produced a tufting machine employing a dozen or more needles, so that a row of tufts six inches or a foot wide could be made at one time. These machines were soon expanded to tuft a row 27 inches wide. Rapidly, they were adapted for use in tufting strips of carpeting, generally on jute.

This represented a very important breakthrough, and a landmark for the carpet industry. The tufting machines were much less expensive than looms, and involved a much simpler process. Because of this, these strips of carpeting could be manufactured at a very much lower price than comparable woven carpeting. Together with one further development—the mass production of synthetic fibres—this was to lead to a revolution in the carpeting industry.

The chemical companies were, at around this time, making many advances in synthetic fibres such as nylon, the acrylics and later, the polyesters. These materials were cheaper than wool, the traditional carpeting material, and had properties which were equal to, and in many cases, superior to wool. After a short period of time, tufting machines were manufactured that could tuft 12 to 15-foot wide carpeting without making strips, in effect the equivalent of 'broadloom' carpeting. But in spite of the obvious potential of this new process, little attention was paid to tufting initially.

A natural conservatism, and the fact that the men who originally began the tufting industry were all without capital, combined to hold up its commercial development. Loans could not be obtained from the banks as the tufters had little equity. The banks would not finance them as that would have entailed relying on the credit of the tufter. But, factors were able to finance the new industry—and did so.

They bought the accounts receivable generated by the tufters, and since they were relying on the credit of the tufter's customers, they did not have to worry about the credit of the tufter himself. In this way, the factors were able to provide working capital for these new companies. The factors also helped in another way, by guaranteeing payment to the tufter's own suppliers the fibre producers. When the fibre was shipped to the tufter, the factor had a security interest in it, and when this was turned into a finished product represented by an account receivable, the factor bought that account receivable and used a portion of the proceeds which he would otherwise have paid to the tufter, to pay the tufter's suppliers. Factoring thus provided a revolving line of credit for the tufting industry which it could not get from other financial sources.

With this assistance, the factor effectively created the tufted carpet industry, an industry that did not exist before 1947. The upshot is that the tufting process has been able to provide carpet equal in quality generally to that produced on looms, but at a significantly lower price. This has enabled millions of consumers in America and elsewhere to buy carpets which they could not previously afford.The carpet industry, which was relatively small after the war, is today selling domestically more than a $1,000M worth of merchandise a year in the U.S. More than 70 per cent is manufactured from man-made fibres, since they are materially less expensive than wool, and more than 90 per cent of that carpeting is tufted.

The reason why the factoring industry was particularly well placed to help the tufters is obvious. The factor, after all, is more concerned than traditional providers of finance with the creditworthiness of a client's customers. He may therefore be less inhibited from taking on clients who are themselves small, but who are selling their products to major industrial and commercial enterprises.

If factoring had existed in Belgium after the war, it might conceivably have provided the means of transforming the Belgian carpet industry from woven to tufted carpeting at a much earlier date, preserving and enlarging the industry in that country. Instead, the advantage that Belgium once had has been lost to other countries. Tufting, today, is now growing strongly in Europe. Mills have been established by large carpet manufacturers in Belgium, Holland, France, Germany, Britain and many other places. Significantly, much of this carpeting volume is being factored, in spite of the fact that most of the companies involved do not suffer from the same financial problems as the early American tufters a quarter of a century ago.

This capacity of factoring to sponsor entirely new manufacturing activities has considerable implications for today's young industries. In a competitive world, the benefits to a country able to exploit new processes, can be large. The pace of technological progress almost daily opens new avenues for the innovator capable of devising fresh or improved products for the consumer market. The very substantial range of new gadgetry stimulated by the advent of the transistor is only one example. If other new industries can be so assisted by factoring, its importance in the expansion of sales and the search for new markets is clearly considerable.

10 The Future of Factoring

Factoring has now a firmly established place in British corporate financing. Increasing awareness of its uses and benefits should ensure that it plays in the future an expanding role in the deployment and conservation of resources. The form its development takes and the size of its contribution, in economic terms, to national output and international trade are less predictable. If the example of American factoring is emulated, the contribution will be considerable. Yet, in many countries it lacks a firm legal foundation, and so long as this state of affairs prevails, its full potential may not be completely realized. Because factoring is a young industry it is still evolving perceptibly. It has emerged at a time of rapid economic change. Indeed, it is partly because of such changes that the need for factoring has arisen, in the same way that the growth of hire purchase and instalment credit was a response to new conditions in earlier years, and other modern techniques like leasing are today also increasing in importance. Inflation, Britain's accession to the European Community, value added tax, wages and prices controls, expanding world trade and an insatiable demand for capital resources are all facets of this changing economic environment.

Almost from its introduction into Britain modern factoring has seemed poised for a dramatic expansion. Actually, its growth and general acceptance has been only gradual. Its comparative high cost (if measured unfairly against traditional and more narrowly based forms of financing) and its early lack of respectability, have combined to impede its growth. But there is now a case for predicting a marked acceleration in factoring business during the coming years.

One reason for this is the commitment of the major clearing banks which in some instances, have deployed substantial resources in the promotion of their factoring offshoots. The banks' participation has not only provided factoring with greater respectability, but will ensure that thousands of branch managers across the country will be both conversant with the factoring technique and able to recommend it in suitable situations. A second reason for expecting a sharp growth in factoring is its obvious application to international trade. This exchange of goods across national frontiers has grown in the last quarter century at a rate unprecedented in the world's economic history.

The dollar value of world exports was increasing during the first half of 1973 at an annual rate of nearly 40 per cent. Even allowing for the affects of currency parity changes and price increases, the volume growth approached 15 per cent. Although this explosive rate of expansion could hardly be expected to be sustained for long, it could, taking one year with another, remain relatively high for some time (in spite of the inevitable setbacks to trade which occur periodically). Britain's accession to the European Community could alone be expected to generate a considerable volume of fresh trade between member states in the medium term. At the same time, any reductions in commercial trade barriers that resulted in coming years from the successful conclusion of multinational trade negotiations, could give a further impetus to the post-war trend. The industrialization programme in many developing countries will also increase the volume of goods exchanged internationally by them. The consequent desire to simplify such transactions will heighten the attractions of factoring. Price inflation, too, could universally stimulate the use of factoring. With inflation in the industrialized world running into double figures companies will increasingly appreciate that the real value of money received on extended credit transactions is rather less than the original price of the goods sold perhaps three months earlier. Again, so long as inflation prevails at such levels, it would seem almost certain that national governments will be forced to adopt stringent wage and price controls. Such controls could, in Britain, become a semi-permanent feature of commercial life, with all the implications that this entails for profit margins and hence capital liquidity.

Moreover, all the evidence suggests that high cost modern technology will in coming years make ever greater demands on a nation's capital resources, creating a much more competitive environment for capital generally. For all these reasons the demand for factoring might be expected to rise. At the same time, in the event of industrial production being curtailed and deflationary economic measures being adopted, the subsequent strain that is inevitably imposed on corporate liquidity also creates a demand for factoring.

For, like religion, factoring can provide a service to suit most circumstances. Clearly, the rate of growth in purchased turnover is slower when the economy is in recession, than when it is expanding. The factor's existing clients are themselves forced to revise downwards their production targets and the commission income of the factor will also be reduced. It is certainly true that the factoring industry overall benefited more strongly from the buoyant economic conditions of 1972–73 than the stagnant conditions of 1970–72. However, a more difficult financial climate can often generate a great deal of new business. Many applicants for factoring will, under these conditions, no doubt be completely undesirable. These are the type of companies that are, in any case, financially weak, with dubious prospects, rocked by the first chill wind that blows through British industry. There will be other applicants, too, not necessarily inherently unsound, but perhaps, with an insufficiently strong management team, or deficient in some other way, that are turned away from the factor's doors. In financially difficult times the foremost need of most applicants will be cash, and the factor will have to be more discriminating than ever in accepting applicants.

But, this ought not to mean that factors are unresponsive to the demands and requirements of the day. Indeed, the responsible factor will be very much aware that at such times he has an important role to play in helping underpin the viable commercial enterprise. One example, which demonstrates just such a situation, occurred during the winter of 1973–74 when the energy crisis, resulting from oil shortages and the coal miners' strike, plunged British industry into the three-day working week. Many factors at that time were actively seeking out companies struggling in the face of the quite exceptional circumstances then prevailing. With output, and consequently earnings, sharply curtailed many firms were confronted with considerable short-term cash problems and required finance to meet labour bills, and the cost of raw materials and overheads. Even though reduced output meant that their raw material requirements were lower than usual, many of their larger suppliers were insisting on cash payments before releasing the stocks needed. Although the cash-hungry company was, in turn, often owed money by its own customers, it was not always possible to effect collections without precipitating the customer's own insolvency. There was thus a threat of a dangerous domino collapse in crucial sectors of British industry, particularly engineering. One contribution that some factors felt able to make was in extending their credit limits for those customers with proven reliability, by 30 days in some cases, to 100 or 120 days. Such a measure can have the effect of easing liquidity pressures right down the manufacturing chain.

By contrast, a downturn in the level of international trade might not be expected, in itself, to have a very significant effect on factoring, at least for some years, as the proportion of this trade conducted by factors is still relatively small. (However, if the downturn was associated with a world-wide recession, the implications would be more profound and the impact on factoring more mixed.) The volume growth of their export-import business would almost certainly slow down if international transactions were declining generally. But the factors' share of this trade might still be expected to grow, even if it did not expand much in absolute terms.

It took some ten years for the total turnover of British factors to reach £200M. Yet, by the end of 1973, it was estimated that the industry's turnover (excluding the non-factoring invoice financers like London Bridge Finance and Goode Durrant & Murray, but including the invoice discounting business of the other factors) was running at around £320M. If LBF and GD & M are included, the total rises to around £400M. Given favourable conditions, it must be more than possible that the industry's turnover—defined as the total value of all clients' invoices handled by the factor—could reach £500M by around 1975–76 and £1,000M by the early 1980s at 1974 values.

If, in 1972, factoring had accounted for 1 per cent of the British gross national product, the industry's turnover would have been more than £600M. A turnover of £1,000M in that year would have represented some 1·6 per cent of G.N.P. If the growth of factoring did no more than keep pace with the expansion of the economy as a whole, and assuming a similar rise in G.N.P. over the period 1972–82 as in the decade 1962–72, then turnover would reach around £650M during that period. If the proportion accounted for by factoring rose from the 0·5 per cent of 1972 to 1 per cent, then turnover would rise to £1,300M. This, of course, constitutes a crude set of calculations, but they are nonetheless indicative of the potential that the industry possesses. At the level of the individual factoring house too, this thesis is borne out. A few factors already have the capacity to cope with hundreds of millions of pounds turnover. Conclusions about the British industry's future turnover cannot, however, be simply drawn from this because in some cases some of this capacity might be utilized to facilitate trade between third countries.

Neither is there any natural limit to the growth of factoring within the British corporate structure itself. At the end of 1972 there were more than 516,000 companies with limited liability status in England and Wales and a further 26,000 in Scotland. Of these 14,000 (1,300 in Scotland) were public companies, the rest being privately owned. In addition, there was a very large, but unknown number of partnerships and small firms without limited liability status.

Therefore, even on the assumption—not necessarily valid—that the largest 100 public companies have less to gain from factoring, at least on their domestic business, and also assuming that a large number of the partnerships and firms will be too small to qualify for its services, there are still probably hundreds of thousands of potential clients. By comparison, perhaps roughly 800 companies were being factored in 1973, a figure which probably rises to more than 1,000 if non-factor invoice discounting is included. Thus, if 10 per cent of the potential factoring market was successfully tapped, this would provide tens of thousands of clients accounting for a sizeable proportion of the national economy.

The only material constraint on the growth of factoring would seem to be a lack of appreciation or awareness of its services. To remedy this many factors have already embarked on educative programmes, holding regular seminars for the uninitiated and expending much energy on increasing public understanding of the industry.

Meanwhile, several trends can already be clearly discerned within the factoring industry's internal structure.Many of those financial institutions only indirectly linked with the industry, and whose involvement was more of a passive financial investment than an active enterprise, have withdrawn: the total number of factoring houses has fallen. Whereas, twelve separate houses have been formed over the course of recent years, (ignoring the smaller provincial factors) the number stood at nine in 1975. Three mergers have taken place within the industry, and little surprise would be caused if others followed.

Factoring is bound to become more sophisticated, more professional and much more competitive. Greater competition will add to the factor's costs or reduce his profit margin. Those houses without some form of direct clearing bank link could find themselves at a disadvantage unless assured both of secure channels of finance and an infrastructure capable of providing a steady stream of new business.

If the American pattern is followed, increasing competition within the factoring industry will exert a considerable downward pressure on commissions. Over some 15 years, from the later 1940s to the middle 1960s, average U.S. factoring commissions were halved, declining from around $1\frac{1}{2}$ per cent to some $\frac{3}{4}$ per cent. This trend is already evident in Britain. Clients are now more inclined to change their factor in the same way they might change their banker. Without the benefits of an expanding turnover and greater operational streamlining, a marked reduction in British factoring commissions could make the business unprofitable for some practitioners. Four out of ten factors suffered trading losses in 1971–72 for various reasons (in one case connected with a client insolvency). Two of these houses have subsequently been merged with other factors. Equally as inflation increases the value of turnover handled, the factor's commissions will rise as they represent a fixed percentage of the higher turnover. Doubtless, there will always be room for the relatively small provincial factors, like Atlas Factors in Glasgow and Century Factors in the West Country, able to capitalize on the specialist knowledge of local conditions and custom to cater for businessmen of the area. But, much of the business is likely to be concentrated in the hands of a limited number of industry leaders, mostly London or South-East-based factors.

Amongst these, too, a certain amount of specialization is predictable. Arguably, the restraints of insufficient capital on an expanding company (often described as the 'MacMillan Gap,' after the report of the MacMillan Committee of 1931, which identified the shortage of long-term external funds as one of the main problems of small, growing companies) begin to bite at a level some way below the £100,000 turnover often currently quoted as a minimum for acceptance by a factor. Because of this, some specialization by factors in companies with a turnover of £40,000 to £100,000, is bound to continue, if not increase.

Furthermore, those factors primarily concerned with the provision of funds (as opposed to the other regular factoring services) might be expected to evolve steadily towards a 'financial package' concept. This envisages a kind of financial 'supermarket' structure, with leasing, factoring, merchant banking and other forms of financing being offered by a single institution. It could ultimately also include stock financing, in the same way that this facility is provided as a natural adjunct to factoring in America.

At the other extreme of the market, the service-orientated factor, perhaps dealing with the larger client, will become steadily more preoccupied with the international markets. The percentage of Britain's factored turnover passing overseas—currently only about 20–25 per cent—should without great difficulty reach 50 per cent, given that roughly this proportion of Britain's manufacturing output is presently exported. For the industrialized world as a whole, only a few hundred million dollars of trade is conducted through the medium of factoring, and it would be surprising if this volume did not expand several fold. However, the degree of economic power that would thus become vested in the hands of the factoring networks could, in some cases, raise delicate questions of national imperatives, for many countries might be chary of seeing such a strategic part of their economies handled by institutions either based in, or controlled from, third countries. More local commercial, if not governmental, participation might rapidly become necessary to assuage such fears.

Problems of this kind could be a particular feature of operations in developing countries where multinational companies are already viewed with considerable suspicion.

There are three other facets of this extension of factoring into the international arena. Firstly, it will very likely stimulate closer links between individual factors across national frontiers, quite independently of those developed through the networks. In this context, the relationship forged between John P. Maguire of America and Credit Factoring International is significant. For this relationship represents a transatlantic partnership between two established factors, rather than just the formation by a multinational factor of yet another new offshoot in a fresh market (albeit, in conjunction with local interests).

Second, it would seem inevitable that international factoring networks will wish to capitalize on the vast store of information that they accumulate, and on their contacts with thousands of importers and exporters around the globe. They will be in a powerful position to match the demands and requirements of their numerous clients, using their commanding advantages not only to facilitate international transactions but actually to generate them. This is already done by the Heller network through its American-based central marketing bureau. Co-ordinating bodies of this type would make it possible to find markets and customers for merchandise, and match specifications, prices and delivery dates, of buyer and seller, with the factor making immediate payment to the exporter and arranging an agreed credit period with the importer.

Finally, at this stage, too, it would seem logical that the factor involve himself more closely in other aspects of this exchange—notably in forwarding freight brokerage and the actual transportation of goods. With a Swedish factor already undertaking forwarding and brokerage for his clients, and another factor linked in the Far East to a steamship company, there are portents to this trend. Such developments on a wide scale would indeed transform the factoring networks into a powerful economic force, although this remains, at the moment, only a distant prospect.

Factors and Value Added Tax

At a more immediate level, the introduction in Britain during April 1973 of value added tax, is not without its significance to the factoring industry. It has, in many cases, proved a boon to clients. For, where the activities of the client did not previously attract purchase tax, his cash advances from the factor are now 10 per cent greater because of higher invoice values. As a consequence, his cashflow has gratuitously benefited. He may, of course, have to pay V.A.T. on his raw materials or components, but while he may not necessarily pay his suppliers for five or six weeks, the extra cash involved in the client's own sales is obtained from the factor shortly after invoices are dispatched. At the same time, the tax attracted by his goods will usually be greater than the V.A.T. paid by him because of the value added by the client's contribution to the finished goods.

All this means that the total value of his debtors would lock up a commensurately larger amount of capital if not converted into cash by the factor. This, naturally, does not apply where the client previously collected purchase tax. Moreover, until the client finally makes the V.A.T. remittance to the Customs and Excise, he will, even when paying his suppliers in cash, have greater sums at his disposal, equivalent to the difference between his tax inputs and outputs. Because of the revolving nature of the tax, he effectively receives a once-and-for-all cash injection. By contrast, the company not factored could, because of V.A.T., face even greater strains on his capital liquidity. Furthermore, taking longer credit from suppliers to help finance this burden, will only intensify the liquidity problems of industry as a whole as each company tries to do the same.

Of course, with V.A.T. payments made to the authorities every calender quarter, most companies will, in any case, begin to accumulate extra funds towards the end of each three-month period, but the extent of this will depend on the particular credit periods that a client's customers take to settle their debts.

However, because invoice values will be inflated by the 10 per cent value added tax, so the higher advances made by factors to their clients will increase the factor's interest charges. For some clients this will be an acceptable cost for the extra funds. But, those clients who do not require the additional cash and who are unwilling to pay the higher interest charge, have the option of simply receiving a lower initial payment. That is, instead of receiving, say, 70 per cent of the higher invoice value (equivalent to 77 per cent of the old debt levels) they will receive around 64 per cent, which would provide them, in money terms, with the same sums as before. In some cases, where the client's V.A.T. accounting and returns are managed by the factor, the benefits of this management might be offset against any increased charges caused by the tax.

International Co-operation

Perhaps the least readily resolvable problem for factoring industries in many countries is the frequently unhelpful legal framework within which they operate. Because factoring has appeared in Europe so recently, national laws do not yet easily accommodate it—indeed, in some cases they are positively hostile. But, equally important, because of the varied national legal traditions and the diverse statutes govering trade payments and titles to accounts receivable, the laws of different countries can sometimes be in conflict. Quite obviously, this is not an unsurmountable problem and in most cases the factor is able to collect payments according to the laws recognized in the debtor's country. It is doubtful if legal problems have in any way served to impede the growth of factoring across frontiers. Yet on the other hand there would seem many advantages in a standardized and simplied system of laws regulating factoring domestically within the main industrialized countries, and internationally. Although on the face of it, this would appear to represent a project of daunting magnitude, it could be achieved either through co-ordinated national enactments or through a multilateral convention along the lines of the 1930 Geneva Treaties on Bills of Exchange, Cheques and Promissory Notes.

Such an objective at present is unrealistic, at least until factoring has become a major force in world trade. In the meantime, it will have to rely on international principles and commercial custom when problems arise. Harmonization within the European Community of the laws of the member states might eventually place all intra-E.E.C. factoring on the same footing. More immediately, an international umbrella organization—a kind of world-wide federation of factors—could help in the formation of guiding principles, ultimately to be embodied in national laws. Nothing remotely resembling such a forum exists at present.

An Association for British Factors

On a more limited scale, co-operation between competing factors has in Britain proved practicable. They were able, for example, to formulate commonly agreed proposals for changes in the law in the wake of the Crowther Committee's report on credit, which were then sent to the Government for further study by officials. However, there was until around the end of 1973, some resistance to a formal association, even though there were successful factors associations in other countries like West Germany. For many years the main point of contact between members of the British industry was the so-called Factors' Club which held informal lunches every couple of months. On these occasions, the general managers of several houses met to discuss mutual problems and exchange views. The Club had a fluctuating membership and no secretariat. The banks who own factors had their own fora for discussions, and resistance to a formal factors' association stemmed from the fear that it would open the way to greater regulation and control from the Government, particularly in times of national credit stringency when the monetary authorities might wish to extend to the factors the kind of rigid ordinances on lending often imposed on other financial institutions. Factors had largely been free from such controls, although the possibility has always existed that bank parents might under certain circumstances be forced to curtail the activities of their factoring offshoots—where they had sufficient control—either at the insistence of the authorities, endeavouring to tighten credit controls, or because they no longer had the available funds.

However, the obvious advantages that a formal trade association could have, seem certain to lead to the formation and registration during 1975 of a body to be called, perhaps, the British Factors' Association (or Association of British Factors). The intention would be that it should broadly resemble in constitution and structure the Finance Houses Association which has a paid secretariat and an elected management committee, together with special sub-committees considering specific issues of interest to the general membership. Like the Finance Houses Association, the British Factors Association has as its main purpose the pursuit of both a legal and economic framework beneficial to the interest of its members, and high professional standards within the industry. It will be in a position not only to help in the collection of better statistics about the factoring industry, but hopefully to achieve a greater influence for its collective voice in Government councils. This could be of particular importance on policies for tackling inflation, controlling aggregate national credit, and reforming the law as it applies to the relationship of borrower and lender.

In the absence of any general reform in this area, or of any specific law addressed to the peculiar characteristics of the factors, uncertainty will continue to prevail and, just conceivably, an adverse court ruling on a point crucial to the factor's security in the purchase of debts, could even bring the British factoring industry to a halt. However, its strength is the proven demand for its services, and this constitutes the best insurance, not only for its continued existence, but of an increasingly important role in the financing of industry and trade. The demand for techniques to liberate scarce resources and lubricate the wheels of commerce is as strong today as it has ever been.

Index